THE SIBLING ARCHETYPE

The Psychology of Brothers and Sisters
and the Meaning of Horizontality

Gustavo Barcellos

SPRING PUBLICATION
THOMPSON, CONN.

The Sibling Archetype: The Psychology of Brothers and Sisters and the Meaning of Horizontality

Published by Spring Publications
Thompson, Conn.
www.springpublications.com

Library of Congress Control Number: 2016947819

ISBN: 978-0-88214-050-6

♾ The paper used in this publication meets the minimum requirements of the American National Standard for Information Sciences — Permanence of Paper for Printed Library Materials, ANSI Z39.48—1992.

Contents

PREFATORY NOTE   5

FOREWORD   9
by Glen Slater

I.   *BROTHERS AND SISTERS*   13
     Fraternal Function — Archetypal Fraternity —
     Transference — Horizontality

II. *THE PSYCHOPATHOLOGY OF*
     SYMMETRICAL RELATIONS   57
     Fraternal Love — Being Wounded by a Sibling:
     Cain and Abel

III. *SIBLINGS AND THE*
     RECONSTITUTED FAMILY   79

…and you are all brothers.
—Matthew 23:8

If, as seems probable, the aeon of the fishes is ruled by the archetypal motif of the hostile brothers, then the approach of the next Platonic month, namely Aquarius, will constellate the problem of the union of opposites.
—C. G. Jung, *CW* 9.2:142

To my sister, Adriana, who helped writing these notes inside me.

Prefatory Note

When some friends and I were considering the idea of organizing an initial meeting in Brazil among our acquaintances and students interested in the discussion of James Hillman's archetypal psychology, back in 2001, it occurred to me that the theme of the siblings, of fraternity, or of horizontal symmetrical relations was a potent catalyst of fantasies that would not only bring about the event we scheduled for that same year but also generate attention to an issue that in many ways seemed relegated to the background of the theoretical concerns of depth psychology—when in my feeling and understanding it should be in the foreground. The reverberations were immense. A vast horizon opened up in the multiple implications that observation and consideration of symmetrical relationships can bring. The topic took firm hold within me and generated reflections that were harder and harder to stay away from.

I saw this topic coming into the most diverse areas of human experience at the beginning of this new millennium, not only in psychotherapy, and I was then able to understand and formulate it into its Jungian designation of the Sibling archetype. Looking for an essentially *psychological* and also profound formulation for fraternity (not theological, nor sociological, nor metaphysical) seemed to me, and still seems, a major challenge to reflection and practice.

I'm not a mythologist, an intellectual, or a professor. I am an analyst trained in psychology, and so the reflections that I propose come from a background that we may call, in all its ambiguity, *soul*, following an ancient psychological and philosophical tradition. These are reflections that stem fundamentally from observation and from the clinic. I follow the method of C. G. Jung that recognizes, as do Joseph Campbell and James Hillman, that myths are found not only in books but also in the streets, in life, and in people's relationships, in the town square, and in the public arena. In other words, in our lives we unconsciously act out those stories, their fictions, and these fictions we call reality. From this perspective, the gods are archetypes of the collective unconscious, cultural and ancestral reserves.

It is from this perspective that I then sought to talk about fraternal love, its hues and paradoxes in individual experience, and about brotherhood as a fundamental field of experiences and action in the world. For the axis of horizontality extends out into the world in all those who we can call brothers and sisters.

Fraternity is not unifying differences; it is differentiating similarities. The experience of alterity is unsettling, challenging, and starts with the siblings. The field of the Other is vast, full of pleasures and pains. Both from the personal point of view and the collective point of view, the possibilities of the Sibling archetype are immense: solidarity, companionship, friendship, associations, cooperation, understanding, loyalty, acceptance. Its wounds are similarly enormous: rivalry, envy, hostility, authoritarianism, civil wars, intolerance, prejudice.

The chapters that comprise this book are the result of the compilation, revision, and expansion of texts written over the past few years, originally presented as contributions to meetings, conferences, or seminars. Gathered here, they outline the small amount of thought I was able to donate to this theme.

—G.B.

Pedra Grande/São Francisco Xavier

February 2009

For the opportunity of having this book published in English translation I wish to acknowledge the importance of my friendship with Margot McLean, Safron Rossi, and Glen Slater, my gratitude to Klaus Ottmann, and my love for Rodrigo Gouvea.

For this English edition, I have revised and expanded the original material, published in Brazil in 2009, so that it could present itself more as a book on the theme of horizontality. What interested me most in this work (and still does) was to go beyond the psychodynamics of brothers and sisters toward an exploration of the metaphor of symmetrical relations and anti-authoritarian horizontality as a possibility for soul-making.

—G.B.

Foreword
by Glen Slater

For those who take the archetypal patterns of the psyche to be primary determinants of the way we live and relate, ground-breaking studies are few and far between. By definition, archetypes form timeless and universal patterns of behavior and imagination. Although their manifestation shows rich variation between cultures and in individuals, the underlying forms are evident in recurring motifs found in myth and religion, art and literature. We thus not so much discover archetypes as rediscover their significance and unearth their psychological implications. In this way, groundbreaking means discerning where the ground of psychological life is being broken open by the force of a previously undervalued archetypal configuration. With this incisive study, *The Sibling Archetype*, Jungian analyst and writer Gustavo Barcellos has achieved just this rare feat.

Barcellos has alerted us to the crucial yet largely obscured role played by brotherhood and sisterhood in the cultivation of soul, throwing light on both a category of intimacy and its mythos in wider realms of human interaction. Reading his extended essay on this topic is like stepping out of a cloud, opening our awareness to the pivotal place these horizontal relationships of equality and mutuality occupy in our lives. From this new standpoint, we can also behold the way vertical, hierarchical relationships, dominated by the dynamics of power and authority, inferiority and superiority, have dominated our thinking. The result is nothing less than a reframing of the relational universe. As Barcellos himself argues, the psychodynamic and metaphorical extension of the sibling pattern into communal and global life promises a "new paradigm" of human interaction and relational values. The democratic impulse, the concern for human rights, the need for ethical awareness and the experience of vital community may all be understood with reference to this archetype.

An important link for Barcellos's perspective appears in a long footnote penned by his mentor and friend, James Hillman, in *The Myth of Analysis* (1972). Hillman was beginning to render Jungian ideas in a new way, moving away from a literal interiority of the psyche toward a recovered sense of soul in the world, proposing the notion of soul-making as a different goal for psychological life. In that key work, Hillman wrote: "If soul-making is the aim, then the equality of the brother-sister relation must be paramount, else eros and psyche cannot constellate." For those who know the history of archetypal psychology, this pivotal placement of the sibling configuration between the notion of soul-making and the primacy of the Eros-Psyche myth is striking. In the chapters of this current work, Barcellos realizes the potential of this insight, showing us how the sibling configuration provides a template for an ensouled mode of existence. This book essentially re-imagines the realm of human interactions in the same way Hillman came to re-vision psychology itself.

Archetypal psychologists will also find in these pages further opportunity for locating the life of the psyche beyond many of the well-worn grooves of early childhood psychodynamics. The overemphasis on vertical relations either directly or indirectly traced to parental figures, which have dominated depth psychological thinking since the early days of Freud and Jung, has long been a critical focus of this approach. In providing a pathway beyond the overbearing claim of the parental fantasy at work in us all, it seems Barcellos offers a more accurate grasp of what actually makes meaning and generates a sense of vitality and significance in everyday life. He writes, "It is with the archetypal Sibling that we construct in our souls the experience and meaning of equality and symmetry, which are so important to success or failure in the various significant relationships we establish during our lives" (76).

Reading this text produces a revelation in which friends and lovers, the experience of community, the familiar bonds of shared circumstances, interests and concerns, and the role of all who inhabit the form of sister and brother, assume a rightful prominence in our psychic landscape. Individuation becomes tied not only to the task of separating from parental influences and their collectivized extensions, but to discerning individual differences among familiars and a sense of other that is rooted in equality. Among siblings and companions of all kinds, we are ushered into a form of knowing and relating through subtle distinctions—"differentiating similarities" (6)—that allows a simultaneous sense of sameness and uniqueness. This opens a stream of consciousness in which nuance, complexity, and "the radical acceptance of difference" (26) can take place—a capacity at the heart of character strength and pervasive wellbeing. By the time Barcellos declares, "the world of soul-making is a horizontal world, not ascendant, not transcendent" (53), he is reminding the psychologist in us all that events and things, and especially the encounter with the other , trump the merely interior or the purely spiritual when it comes to the generation of soul.

Barcellos is a well-known psychotherapist in his native Brazil, where he leads seminars, writes on archetypal psychology, and has translated a large number of Hillman's writings into Portuguese. Whereas we may expect a certain vertical depth of thought from such an experienced Jungian, the kind of horizontal depth of vision and relational acuity articulated in these pages is hardly common. Yet, not only is it present here as a vivid grounding for these psychological reflections, it is something thoroughly evident in the author's approach to those who have come to know him. As many who have worked and studied with him will attest, his capacity for the kind of comradery, friendship, and brotherly bonding articulated in these pages has created a genuine community for archetypal explorations. Of all the things to acknowledge on the threshold of this work, the congruence between its themes and the author's character is the most apparent. Barcellos is not only an engaging colleague and a generous scholar, he is a warm host and a firm friend. As you enter into the perspective that follows, I hope you can imagine him sitting down with you, sharing his masterful reflections on just this art of companionship and dialogue, from which much of the soul-making process emanates.

I. *Brothers and Sisters*

> We are that pair of Dioscuri, one of whom is mortal and
> the other immortal, and who, though always together,
> can never be made completely one.
> – C. G. Jung

Fraternal Function

With the term "fraternal function" I not only call forth my
topic, invoking our imagination and calling upon our soul, but
from the outset I provoke while suggesting that the similar, the
"sibling," has a structural impact, or is even *necessary* in the
constitution of individuality, or in what Jungians most widely
call individuation. If this is the case, then the mental image or
symbol of the "brother/sister" *functions,* and functions in a certain way, with an end determined by the soul. Here I follow the
meaning that C.G. Jung gave to the term *function* as a process
in time that acts, operates, performs.[1] However, I also understand *function* to be something that operates with the backing
of a suprapersonal, extrarational instance of collective nature,

---

1. "The term is used in the meaning of operation or activity, which is
the most recurring both in scientific and common language... Through
these expressions [functions], psychic activities of a dynamic nature
and which are subject to education are always indicated." Paolo Francesco Pieri, *Dicionário junguiano* (São Paulo: Paulus, 2002), 213.

in other words, by an *arché*, a primary principle, the archetypal reality Jung called *archetype*—in the case of the fraternal function and sibling relations, namely, *Fratria*.

The decline or the weakening of the archetypal image of the father in the imagination of contemporary societies, the father who is absent from the culture, confronts in psychology the enormous and pervasive presence of the Mother archetype in its theories and practices. Archetypal psychology has shown this in its reflection on psychology itself. "When the father is absent, we fall more readily into the arms of the mother," said James Hillman.[2] The Mother is everywhere. The first formulations of Jungian theory have to do with imagining the development of personality through the lenses of the great metaphor of the hero's battle against the seduction of the dragon of matter—where matter, mother, and the unconscious are all equivalent. Later, alchemy disrupted and redesigned this scenario for Jung. But it is to her, to the Mother, that the notions of healing, development, evolution and growth, adaptation, and the unconscious belong, even today. Succumbing to her, as *son*, or beating her, as *hero*, are the alternatives of a helpless soul—and individual facets, in our culture, of the matter/spirit relationship.

In choosing the fraternal archetype as a theme, I indicate the need to escape the maternalism and paternalism, which are already far too present and exploited in our psychological imagination. I wish to draw attention to the diversity and richness of horizontal relationships—the first subjective paradigm of which is the sibling. This suggests a reflection where the hierarchical or vertical family perspective symbolized by the parent-child relationship gradually yields, in the culture and in

---

2. James Hillman, *Senex & Puer*, Uniform Edition of the Writings of James Hillman (*UE* hereafter), 11 volumes (Putnam and Thompson, Conn.: Spring Publications, 2004 -), 3: 121.

the individual, to a more equalized brother-sister perspective. This also means refining the concepts of *similarity in difference,* not only in individual psychology, but also in social and political spheres. It also means imagining the psychological clinic as a work that can constellate and be marked by the horizontal transferences of fraternity. I think that psychology also must follow the movement that has been detected in other arts and sciences: the current search for the paradigm of horizontality. Psychoanalysis, with its three patriarchs—Freud, Jung, and Adler—opened last psychological century with a focus on parental relationships: Oedipus, the hero, and the family. This model has begun to be criticized and revised. The transition to the new millennium could open the twenty-first century with the task of focusing on fraternal symmetrical relationships.

The fundamental role of the Sibling archetype in structuring and establishing individual adult life is undeniable, yet still dismissed. Brothers and sisters are powerful figures in our lives as we build our mature relationship patterns. The patterning of all our relationships with friends and lovers comes from our experience as siblings. Here, the main lesson is equality. Curing the eternal wounds created in these relationships is a lifelong task, since these relationships accompany us throughout our lifetimes. However, it is clear that depth psychology and culture in general have neglected a more detailed observation and theoretical reflection on this topic, and instead have focused more intensely on the relationships we build with mothers and fathers. In our field, the rather complete *Dicionário junguiano,* for example, which was edited in Italy by Paolo Francesco Pieri (along with the main dictionaries, lexicons, and reference works in the area of Jungian psychology[3]), do not contain the

---

3. The exception is Daryl Sharp's *Jung Lexicon: a Primer of Terms and Concepts* (Toronto: InnerCity Books, 1991), which contains a (small) entry for "Hostile brothers": "An archetypal motif associated with the

entry "Brother/Sister." This is part of the shadow where these relationships are found in psychology.

Nevertheless, as a primordial image in the soul, the sibling is present and active in the psychological evolution of each individual (even the only child) and each culture, and its influence is inevitably projected in the history and in the construction of bonds with friends, companions, partners, and colleagues.

There are several types of brother/sisterhood. The *brother/sister* type is, in the first and most basic sense of the word, a child of the same father and the same mother. But with relation to other children there is also the *consanguine brother,* as we call the child who is the son of only the same father, and the so-called *uterine brother,* the son of only the same mother. There are the *twin brothers*: multiples of the same or different sexes, identical or fraternal twins, those that look the same or completely different; and the *Siamese twins*, individuals who are physically inseparable. [4] There are the *milk brothers* (milk

---

opposites constellated in a conflict situation. Examples of the hostile-brothers motif in mythology are the struggle between Gilgamesh and Enkidu in The Gilgamesh Epic, and the Biblical story of Cain and Abel. Psychologically, it is generally interpreted in terms of the tug of war between ego and shadow" (61-62).

4. The term "siamese twins" (conjoined twins) is a reference to the most famous pair of twins in modern history, Chang and Eng Bunker, who were born in Siam (now Thailand) in 1811. Though they shared the same liver, they lived as independent a life as they could. At that time it was impossible to separate them. They were for a long time exhibited as a curiosity on world tours. They ended up living in Wilkesboro, North Carolina, and married local women, the sisters Adelaide and Sarah Yates. As the wives began to dislike each other in later years, they set up separate households, and would then alternately spend half of the time at each wife's home. They fathered a total of twenty-one children. They are said to have had distinct personalities, Eng being sweet and calm, while Chang used to drink heavily and was temperamental. At the end of their lives they quarreled

kinship), who were breastfed by the same woman, despite being the biological children of different mothers. And then there are *brothers raised together,* raised in the same household without being biological brothers. The *adopted brother* may be part of a mixed composition where the parents have one or more biological children, the *real brothers,* or a unique constellation comprised exclusively of adopted children. There are also the *brothers-in-arms,* war companions. And with respect to reconstituted families, we can mention the *stepbrother,* who is the son who comes along with the new spouse, and the *half-brother,* the son of the new couple.

So many arrangements. The archetypal image of the sibling in the psyche—the *soul brother* or *soul sister*—brings together all these modalities and makes them metaphors for potential future formats for our relationships with others and with the world. Models of horizontality.

Certainly, the radicalization of the idea of *fratria* strongly affects our clinical practice, but even more, it affects our love for the world. The presence of the fraternal archetype, its need, and its action, is ever more clear, just as much in the social area, where institutionalized actions on the part of the State are increasingly yielding to more independent nonofficial significant actions, and are increasingly important in the different forms of solidarity. An example of this is the proliferation of the work of NGOs (Non-Governmental Organizations) in a variety of spheres of public life and the common human experience (especially in Latin America). NGO's are structures of solidarity. Psychology and the art of psychotherapy are also moving toward a new paradigm, although this is not easily perceived. The resistance to this movement is the sign

---

a lot. Chang died on 17 January 1874 while the brothers were asleep. Eng woke up in shock and died approximately three hours later. They were 63 years old.

of a faded and exhausted practice, as the first patriarchal century of psychoanalysis comes to a close. This new paradigm,
I believe, has to do with the Sibling archetype.

However, the years of study devoted to understanding the
issues that provoke me the most in Jungian psychology, allow-
ing me to add the deepening and the re-visioning that the perspective of James Hillman's archetypal psychology brings,
have made me sensitive to a large gap: the almost total absence
of images, in the literature and in practice, of the theoretical
apparatus that could permit the recognition and understanding, throughout its entire reality, of the importance and the
impact of nonhierarchical horizontal fraternal relations in the
daily work of the psyche, whether in the individual or in collective spheres. A resounding affirmation is found in a footnote in Hillman's 1972 book, *The Myth of Analysis,* that pointed
in this direction and today is the motive for this book:

> Mother-son (Oedipus) and father-daughter (Electra)
> ex-pose only half of the dual conjunction; where con-
> cern for soul is paramount, a relationship takes on
> more the nature of the brother-sister pair. Compare
> the *soror* in alchemy and the appellations of "Brother"
> and "Sister" in religious societies... if soul-making is
> the aim, then the equality of the brother-sister rela-
> tion must be paramount, else eros and psyche cannot
> constellate. Paternalism and maternalism become
> clinically unsound if soul-making is the aim. [5]

Those statements have had a profound impact on me since
my first reading of this powerful note back in 1984. What
surprised me most then, and still does today, was that such a
relevant and strong understanding of a new yet still unnoticed
paradigm—not only for psychology, but for culture as well—this

---

5. James Hillman, *The Myth of Analysis: Three Essays in Archetypal Psychology* (New York: Harper & Row, 1978), 57n56.

Aquarian fantasy of horizontality, symmetry, and the importance of nonhierarchical connections, was presented in a footnote, that is, in a somehow marginal position, in the borders
of reflection, not in the main text. The repression of horizontality was in a way also showing here. I wanted to understand
this repression.

Nonetheless, the wealth of images is all there and available
in the myths, the fairy tales, the stories, and the clinic. Our
topic is very broad. I nevertheless have just a few questions,
some incomplete speculations, a free thought that I shall begin
to formulate.

The first and perhaps most crucial questions are: what is
the true impact of the fraternal function on individuation,
as it is presented in the symbolic appearance of the brother/
sister—whether this is literally determined through blood ties
or not? How can this soul sibling (who is more than simply
the Other, a stranger, the Shadow) determine, or influence, or
ordain the maturing of my individuality and my action in the
world? I wish to think that the sibling, as the significant Other,
defines my being in the world and my love for the world at levels beyond those of mother and father. How, then, does one
become sensitive to these levels in the work *of* the soul and in
work *with* the soul? How does one differentiate an archetype
like this one, the one of *Fratria,* in its formative and deformative
aspects, to the point that we would understand the individual
completely from this standpoint—in other words, based in *its*
key in the psychic body and the body politic—without falling
back into the arms of the Mother and the concerns with origin,
with causality?

An active interest on the brother/sister helps relativize and
resize the importance and tremendous influence, conscious or
unconscious, that the Mother figure has in our lives. Escap-
ing the Mother signals a new paradigm for the process of self-
knowledge and self-realization that no longer passes through

that reductive understanding that sees the most important explanation and the stronger and more efficient causes always in the *origins* of things. Interest in fraternal relations also helps us to escape from the Father and the dangers that appear in the numinous shadow of this figure: remaining a child, dependent, tangled up in questions of authority and submission.

From an archetypal perspective, the sibling impact also goes beyond, on the one hand, that which was already formulated in Jungian psychology as the "projection of the shadow," that is, the projection of the unlived life: themes of conflict, opposition or complementarity, which often explain the fraternal discord that appears in the mythological origin of so many civilizations. This is the archetypal theme of sibling rivalry, emphasized by Freud and by Jung. Jung so often referred to the shadow as the "inner brother." So it would free us from experiencing the fraternal archetype only through the lenses of the shadow.

And, on the other hand, it goes beyond the contrasexual psychodynamics of *anima* and *animus* that are especially projected on the brother-sister pair, where the sister is a powerful image for the adult male, reconnecting him with his inner world of feelings in a less threatening way than the overwhelmingly numinous *imago* of the Mother.[6] So, for me, interest in the Sibling archetype and its phenomenology would free us from a psychology still dominated by contrasexual imaginings.

This "sibling impact," as I call it, translates more psychologically into the experience of real perception, assimilation, and appreciation of *diversity*. The first and founding experience of diversity, of similarity in difference, which is established when

---

6. "The mother is superior to the son, but the sister is his equal." C.G. Jung, *Psychology and Alchemy*, Collected Works of C.G. Jung, trans. R.F.C. Hull, 20 volumes (Princeton, N.J.: Princeton University Press, 1953-79, *CW* hereafter and cited by paragraph number), 12: 92.

a sibling appears (again, either through a blood tie or through a bond of friendship), is important precisely to the extent that it allows us to relativize the monotheistic identification with the model of paternal authority, throwing us into the polytheistic field of horizontal relationships that permits free movement between valid ethical singularities. That underlies to me the very Jungian idea of individuation, that is, *differentiation.*[7]

This Other-Brother/Brother-Other, the sibling, sisters and brothers, the similar who is not the same, but is a peer (and later there will be many peers, many Others), is another who shares my exact same origin. In other words: the same people, or *that* (as founding principles), that fathers and mothers this Other are the same that fathers and mothers me. And yet, he/she is different. Is this not, for the soul, an initiation into diversity in the closest and most immediate manner? I believe that the modes of this initiation unfold in all subsequent commitments between the peers, agreements between brothers, the civilizing pact, what we may call *ethics.*

As an archetype, *fratria* naturally extends beyond the literal experience with brothers and sisters. And in both the presence and absence of siblings, *fratria,* soul brother/sisterhood, tends to unfold and color the relationships we have in our adult lives, our relationships with the world, and even with nature. For on an archetypal level, brotherhood is the foundation of the feeling of friendship. *Philia* (Latin for "friendship") not only emerges from but also deepens *fratria. Fratria* is *philia*'s matrix, and this is exactly what allows us to understand the bonds of elective friendship as fraternal ties that ultimately fall within the logic of this archetype. These ties are the expression of an *eros* that Plato understood to be the highest level of love. In this way, the Sibling archetype seems to be a wide field

---

7. "Individuation, therefore, is a process of differentiation." Jung, *Psychological Types, CW* 6: 757.

of affective experiences where the closest friends, intimate friends, appear and are so often called "brothers."

However, the relationship with the blood brother/sister brings the particularity and the feeling of something that is given with destiny, that is meant to be. It is permanent and is not, initially, a link of dependency, as with the father and mother; and it is not chosen, as best friends are. The relationship with the brother/sister builds the emotional foundation and affective model for other intimate horizontal relationships we establish in adult life, as I have been suggesting, which often brings to individuation the hard task of re-establishing or rebuilding broken relationships with our actual brothers and sisters. At this level, it is with them that we learn to get along.

When questioned, however, the bond with siblings almost always appears problematic, or neglected. This situation—of detachment, distance, silence, or even voluntary separation, hatred and rancor—is so often seen in clinical psychotherapy, as well as when talking to friends and acquaintances. It is intriguing and points to a very deep unconscious wound. I will try to reflect on this wound in Chapter 2. In no other relationship are the emotional paradoxes of intimacy and distance, far and near, equal and different, so categorically ardent, so apparent, so immediate.

Siblings guard our memory, are witnesses of our lives, and are so often present at our birth and our death—a relationship, perhaps the only one, that may be lifelong. With them we share our formative years. In other words, siblings are our *familiars*, and this might be the most important: they are at the base of what makes it possible for us to become *familiar* with something or someone, to *familiarize* as a process in which we become intimate, known and knowledgeable, related.

Secondly, I think we should dedicate an effort to releasing our notions of fraternity, on one hand, primarily from its most recent roots in the ideals of the French Revolution, where the liberty-equality-fraternity triad was created as the first expression, in the modern world of culture, of the longing to surpass the Father as a paradigm of relations and authority: regicide, the refusal of the paternal *imago,* the revolutionary orphanhood that archetypically aims horizontality. This conceptual modern triad is the secular version of the Christian triad. Although not a legal category, fraternity becomes the principle that should rule over the civil relations between people. And fraternity is not independent from liberty and equality, for the three inform each other mutually. The French Revolution conception of equality opposes it to hierarchy and tyranny; its idea of liberty permits the conception of diverse subjectivities and the very idea of the individual.

If we examine a simple, encyclopedic summarization of French Revolution, we can see it is all there:

> French Revolution (1789). A complex upheaval, profoundly affecting every aspect of government and society, and therefore considered a significant turning point in French history...with wide sweeping political, social, and economic measures (1789-91). These included the abolition of feudal, aristocratic, and clerical privileges, the Declaration of the Rights of Man, the establishment of a constitutional government, the confiscation of church estates, and the reorganization of church-state relations in the Civil Constitution of the Clergy (1790). Thus the *ancien régime* was effectively dismantled in the name of liberty, equality and fraternity...[8]

The Revolution culminated in a fundamental document, passed by France's National Constituent Assembly in August

---

8. *The Cambridge Encyclopedia of the English Language,* ed. David Crystal (Cambridge: Cambridge University Press, 1995).

1789, the "Declaration of the Rights of Man and of the Citizen" (*Déclaration des droits de l'homme et du citoyen*). The Declaration defined a set of individual and collective rights for men, insisting on *liberty* and *equality* — social and political rights held to be universal and valid in all times and places, as it is stated in the first article of the Declaration: "Men are born and remain free and equal in rights. Social distinctions can be founded only on the common good." This Declaration was also a major inspiration for the important "Universal Declaration of Human Rights," adopted by the United Nations General Assembly on 10 December 1948. It consists of thirty articles that have been elaborated in subsequent international treaties. It is profoundly influenced by the fraternal archetype, as (again) its very first Article makes clear: "All human beings are born free and equal in dignity and rights. They are endowed with reason and conscience and should act towards one another in a spirit of brotherhood."

But, on the other hand, we should also free fraternity from the Christian tradition, older in time and deeper in the soul. Christianity has notoriously absorbed the idea of fraternity into a monotheistic environment, as we know, connecting it especially to the notion of charity. *Fratria,* as any archetype, is naturally subjected to historically ideological absorptions and actualizations. But here, more than anywhere else, we need to see through: *fratria* as an archetype is a possibility and a *state of the soul*; again, a *function* in the soul that, if seen psychologically, is complex by its very nature, leading us — whether externally (politically) or internally (individually) — to the multiple democratic challenges of community and of horizontal coexistence. We can then face the Christian notion of fraternity as an exercise in the *arché* of the *fratria*.

According to Apostle Peter, fraternity is the type of union that should characterize the relationships of truly Christians: "Honour all men. Love the brotherhood. Fear God. Honour the King" (1 Peter 2:17). Christianity brings to the center the idea of fraternity: all men and women are brothers and should treat each other as such. The Christian conception of fraternity means loving the Other; for Christianity, Jesus came to make fraternity possible, to make us all brothers: "But be not ye called Rabbi: for one is your Master, even Christ; and ye are brethren" (Matthew 23:8). The true relation between all men is that of brothers.

The word "brother" appears 347 times in the New Testament. It defines the universal community of men, and nobody is excluded: "For by one Spirit are we all baptized into one body, whether we be Jews or Gentiles, whether we be bond or free; and have all been all made to drink into one Spirit" (1 Corinthians 12:13); "For whom he did foreknow, he also did predestinate to be conformed to the image of his Son, that he might be the firstborn among many brethren" (Romans 8:29).

Although the word—fraternity—can sometimes be mistaken for charity or solidarity, in its strict Christian sense it refers to a sentiment or deep feeling that should in fact be called *agapē* (mutual love): a kind of love that leads humanity to a sense of spiritual community founded on love for each other, a community of equals, or brothers/sisters. For Christians, friendship (*philia*) is not enough: we need brotherly love (*fratria*).

But the Christian conception of fraternity and fraternal love is entirely built in relation to the Father, one common Father that, with His presence and His love, establishes brotherhood among His children. His love is what makes us brothers and sisters. An authentic and true fraternity supposes and demands paternity; it is tied to the Father.

Then, what we need now is a conception of fraternity where brothers/sisters constitute themselves as brothers/sisters without the need for the hierarchical asymmetrical reference to a Father for its base and meaning. I suggest that we need now to construct a *psychological* meaning for this word, *fraternity*, considering it through its archetypal dimension, where, at its limits of light and shadow, fraternity would point toward both the radical acceptance of difference, as well as the need to comprehend the paranoid repulsion of the Other.

In third place: the important question of authority. How to consider it, or to reconsider it, in a panorama between siblings? What authority is this that could be exercised without an investment in the Father figure? Is it possible to experiment with authority *without* the archetypal investment of the Father figure? What authority would this then be? Would it have more to do with authorship, and therefore, with *authorizing* oneself?

Well, here we would have a self-authorization that no longer means the introjection of the Father, that would no longer be imagined in this way, as in the classical Jungian formulation: internal activation of the archetypal father, naturally updated in the historical father, in the paternal complex, in the complexities of the paternal, in the complex authority. But instead, we would be *authorized to authorize ourselves*.

For modern individuality, this would mean rescuing the Father now as *dysfunction,* something that no longer works in accordance with the needs of the soul, or that which Freudians refer to as the murder of the Father of the primeval horde to establish an order among siblings.[9]

We should bear in mind that at the origins of depth psychology stands Freud — the Father of psychoanalysis — choosing Oedipus (or is it Oedipus choosing Freud?), Oedipus as the supreme paradigm of subjectivity, the key to the soul, the very "soul's code." And that, by choosing him, Freud mythically emphasized patricide, mythical patricide, and with it the hierarchical family, or the family hierarchy, or family *as* hierarchy, and, of course, fatherhood. With Freud we embark

---

9. Sigmund Freud, *Totem and Taboo* (1913).

incestuously on a family romance to understand the human soul, securing it a psychodrama of origins—which, in itself, is no less than a mythologizing movement.

And even though James Hillman, in his most significant 1987 essay, "Oedipus Revisited,"[10] alerts us to the fact that what is at stake, or on stage, in the Oedipus tragedy is *infanticide,* not patricide—because that desire to kill the child comes *before* and determines all the tragic action—it seems he is just reverting the vectors: we are still tragically involved in the curse of the vertical family circus/theater to experience, or "decipher," psychological depth. There is no place for siblings.

The little that was observed and pondered by Freud and Jung regarding fraternal relations was from the reference to a family model that in many places is almost entirely extinct (of course, there are exceptions). Other formats, models and designs for family relationships and parenting arrangements, the "new families," gradually are seen to draw closer to this traditional model other ways of doing and experimenting this nucleus called *family.* Separated parents, with other children in other homes, remarry with other partners, often with other children from unions with these new partners (often with wide age gaps) and sometimes half-brothers, as we call the blended family; adopted children (often also among non-adopted siblings); only children of a union are raised by grandparents, aunts and uncles, or educators, far from the parent's home; the family of gay men (where children, whether adopted or biological, are raised by homosexual couples); the lesbian family (often with children fathered by gay men); the family headed by a single mother or father; or the complex situation of children who find themselves having to replace or help an absent mother or father (or a parent who is overloaded with tasks in a numerous family), bringing a more parental role to the family

10. James Hillman, "Oedipus Revisited," in *Mythic Figures, UE* 6.

landscape;[11] and so many other examples that we can highlight or even imagine and predict, from monoparental to homo-parental and multiparental families (showing ever more clearly that family is not a phenomenon of nature but of culture) — all this certainly has a significant psychological impact on the arrangement of light and shadow, love and hate, cooperation and distancing in fraternal relationships.

The observations I am now trying to make refer us to the deeper meanings of *family* and *familiar*. The play on words in this case is intense, and naturally reveals more complex meanings. It is important not to forget that this archetypal unit that we modern Westerners call *family* derives from a Latin idea that primarily meant the house and all that belonged to it, or that was in it, as well as movable and immovable property, furniture and belongings, inhabitants and guests, animals and things, as well as its heritage and ancestry, an idea originally linked to the land itself or to the place where it was located. A structure that has its main archetypal base in the ideas of "shelter," "protection." Belonging to a family, or even when something or someone becomes familiar, echoes this imaginatively deeper and wider sense: becoming familiar, or known and intimate, includes the world.

I think that it is the sibling, maybe even more intensely than any other figure, who determines the development of our psychological capacity of *familiarity* and *symmetry,* that is, the ability to approach things and experiences in a familiar manner, to eventually make them intimate. This only happens when we learn the intrinsic value of symmetrical relations, or when these are not plunged into the shadows of unconsciousness.

---

11. An excellent expansion on this theme can be seen in Mariette Mignet, "La grande soeur," *Cahiers Jungiens de Psychanalyse* 101: *Frères et Soeurs* (Summer 2001): 7-20.

Moreover, in the family, the parents are somehow responsible for offering or taking away from the children the experience of symmetrical horizontal relations, since it is with them that the foundation and the actual possibility for the emergence of these relationships appear. The parents can, for example, be quite absorbing in a family environment and teach only hierarchical patterns of relationships. This may already be present in the couple, of course, but also is strengthened in the range of collusions and alliances that each parent may more or less unconsciously have with one of the children. These identifications and alliances do not liberate; on the contrary, they darkly imprison the meaning and experience of symmetry.

The same important passage from James Hillman's 1972 book, *The Myth of Analysis,* to which I have already referred to earlier, allows us to see these issues of family and brotherhood/sisterhood even more sharply. Here it is worth examining some excerpts of this long quote that nonetheless appears in a footnote (again, note that it is highly significant that, even here, these issues are kept on the sidelines, left at the foot of the page, in a peripheral, marginal condition, even in the work of the person who I believe best intuited them in our field):

> To the alarm of moralists and sociologists, the nineteenth-century model of the family is disintegrating. When this problem of the family is conceived only through the Oedipus myth, not only is it old hat, but the family complex becomes insoluble and family life insupportable, necessitating the myth of the hero whose journey toward consciousness leads away from home. But we cannot go home again, not even as repentant prodigals. Nor can we moderns, whose consciousness is characterized by uprootedness, exile, and an "anti family" bias, attempt to restore a model of the nineteenth-century family by repeating it in our lives. The reconstitution of the family can be based on neither the former metaphor of parent and child nor

the new one of a democratic "functional" family. To recreate family in our generation, eros and psyche must have the possibility of meeting in the home; this would favor soul-making and give an altogether different perspective to family relationships. This perspective looks less to the hierarchical connections of parent-child and the issues of early childhood, authority, and rebellion and more to the soul connection, as between brother and sister. Mother-son (Oedipus) and father-daughter (Electra) expose only half of the dual conjunction; where concern for soul is paramount, a relationship takes on more the nature of the brother-sister pair. Compare the soror in alchemy and the appellations of "Brother" and "Sister" in religious societies. Compare also the symbolic interrelations in the *I Ching*, where six of the eight hexagrams are "sons" and "daughters," which, to one another are brothers and sisters. Kinship libido, which, as Jung points out, is behind incest phenomena, would flow on the brother-sister model into mutuality of soul-making rather than regressively toward parents. As J.E. Harrison says (*Prolegomena to the Study of Greek Religion* [Cambridge, Eng., 1922], p. 655), Eros is also the dance, and the dance is not a hierarchical phenomenon. It takes place between the partners. The implications for psychotherapy of the family problem are obvious: if soul-making is the aim, then the equality of the brother-sister relation must be paramount, else eros and psyche cannot constellate. Paternalism and maternalism become clinically unsound if soul-making is the aim. [12]

For a footnote, we can agree, it is enormous, and it is not even reproduced here in full; it's almost a "parallel essay" in the book. But it is enough for what interests us here. Yes, the

12. Hillman, *The Myth of Analysis*, 57n56.

"implications" are obvious: here, symmetrical relationships are ultimately shown as most conducive to soul-making itself, to the work of "making" or cultivating soul, understood in this way in its most advanced paradigm. This paradigm is the reunion of Eros and Psyche in psychological life, love and soul, as archetypal psychology has already proposed in the essays of this same book by Hillman.

I wish now to highlight two statements contained in this footnote that best reflect the thought that I am seeking to enter here: "where concern for soul is paramount, a relationship takes on more the nature of the brother-sister pair"; and, "if soul-making is the aim, then the equality of brother-sister relationship must be paramount." These thoughts suggest that interest in soul, therefore, depends strongly on a *relationship of equality*, a relationship of symmetry, in the horizontal plane. These are important statements that definitely expand our theme. It seems to me that it is therefore in the fraternal relations, in a broad and metaphorical sense, that is to be found the most fertile, deep, and creative field to advance a concern, a care, and a sense of soul in our lives, its processes, and its wounds. I believe this is so because of the horizontality proper to fraternal/symmetrical relationships, its ability to constellate equality and difference at the same time, its nonhierarchical paths, and the inherent difficulties that directly result from its symmetric field.

Although we can understand Hillman's statements as clear indications of the importance of horizontal relations in general for the deepest work with soul, he nonetheless explicitly refers mainly to the brother-sister pair, that is, the pair of opposite-sex siblings. We know that the pair of same-sex siblings contains, in addition to what Hillman already indicates, still other specific aspects of the fraternal relations, which notably would help us elaborate a psychology of brotherhood and of sisterhood—as we can specially find in Christine Downing's book,

Psyche's Sisters,[13] where she argues that our deepest psychological bonds are to be found in same-sex relationships.

Jung also had already understood the image of brother-sister incest in alchemy as one of the most powerful images of the psyche, as a symbol of the ultimate union of opposites, relating it to creation itself:[14] "It represents the union of two equals on the same kinship level unlike mother/son or father/daughter."[15] Jung also states that, since the most remote times, this image has been nothing less than the "prototype of the alchemist's great work" (*Mysterium Coniunctionis, CW* 14:735). "The brother-sister pair stands allegorically for the whole conception of opposites" (*CW* 12: 436), he further states in *Psychology and Alchemy,* understanding their central place in the work. Every alchemist reproduces this archetypal background on the human plane because he almost always works with a helper called his *soror mystica,* his soul sister, the artifice's companion. Jung lists famous pairs: Simon Magus and Helena, Zozimos and Theosebeia, Nicholas Flamel and Lady Perenelle (the most famous and perfect *soror,* wife of Flamel, the great French alchemist, who helped him in creating the stone, which it is said they achieved at least twice). It is a clear indication of what is most conducive to soul-making, which is emerging, according to Jung, symbolically in the Sun/Moon pair. The importance of the *soror mystica* is also quite apparent, for example, on the figures of the *Mutus Liber,*

---

13. Christine Downing, *Psyche's Sisters: Re-Imagining the Meaning of Sisterhood* (New Orleans: SpringJournal Books, 2007).

14. "The alchemical union of opposite forces and substances in the chemical wedding is often portrayed as an incestuous union... The incestuous *coniunctio* is most frequently represented as the union of brother and sister." Lyndy Abraham, *A Dictionary of Alchemical Imagery* (Cambridge: Cambridge University Press, 1998), 106.

15. Brian Clark, *The Sibling Constellation: The Astrology and Psychology of Sisters and Brothers* (Arkana: Penguin Books, 1999), 72.

the known series of alchemical engravings from 1677, where she is almost always present.

A powerful image of the brother-sister pair can also be found in the marriage of Zeus and Hera as a mythical pattern in the Greek tradition. This mythological brother-sister marriage has a sacred character, it is a true *hieros gamos,* and in its symbolic meaning, due to their being siblings, represents the deep equality and companionship that are archetypally given in every marriage.

It is thus the brother-sister pair—which is, of course, a clear allusion to symmetry—that appears here as the essential image in psychological working. But here, again, symmetry perceived or referred to as essential to soul-making (as in Jung and Hillman) is to be mainly found in an opposite-sex pair. The brother and sister marriage presents an image of intense intimacy, no doubt, and as such it stands for an image of wholeness, but this is essentially an image of wholeness as union with oneself, not with the Other. This is the union of ego and *anima,* of consciousness and unconscious, as if still in a vertical environment. It is marriage with one's own soul. In this strange couple, the royal marriage of Brother/King and Sister/Queen, with all its erotic charge and bizarre alchemical imagery, Jung saw a symbol of the Self, that is, an image for the encounter with oneself. We need to move on to the next step: "the importance of same-sex relationships as images for psychic wholeness."[16] Jung writes in *Mysterium Coniunctionis*:

> ...the marriage symbolism obviously never quite satisfied the alchemical thinkers themselves, since they constantly felt obliged to make use of other "uniting symbols," besides the numerous variants of the hierosgamos...thus the *coniunctio* is represented by the dragon embracing the woman in the grave, or

---

16. Downing, *Psyche's Sisters,* 134.

by two animals fighting, or by the king dissolving in water, and so on.[17]

The mutuality of soul-making can also be expressed and lived, with all its specific characteristics, in images of deep union of brothers with brothers and sisters with sisters. Downing notes that "in many human societies it is taken from granted that the most intimate human bonds will be with same-sex others."[18] This same-sex mutuality would certainly point to a deeper understating of soul-making.

One last free speculation to end this chapter. Would Westerners be more archetypically oriented toward horizontality, from what can be perceived as a psychic logic as it is reflected in the logic of writing, since in Western languages the sentences are written horizontally? We write from left to right, as I am doing right now—while in some Asian languages (Chinese and Japanese, for example) writing is done from top to bottom. There may be some mysterious, unconscious relation between this horizontality, this passion for horizons, this avocation for the infinite of horizontality in the soul's search for depth and our theme, the Sibling archetype.

Archetypal Fraternity

Fraternity: fraternities, brotherhoods, associations, societies, sororities, clubs, clans, partnerships, fellowships, groups, associations, unions, communities, *thiasos*. Blood ties, blood pacts. Sects, sectarianism. Sibling rivalry, sibling fights. In the dictionary, "fraternity," noun, has the following definitions: "a group of people associated or formally organized for a common purpose, interest, or pleasure"; "the quality or state of being brothers"; and "persons of the same class, profession,

---

17. Jung, *Mysterium Coniunctionis*, *CW* 14: 669.
18. Downing, *Psyche's Sisters*, 116.

character, or tastes."[19] Meanwhile, the adjective fraternal brings a sense of affection. This fraternal feeling can be found in brothers, friends, partners, associates, comrades, coworkers, and even in the "hey bro."

Fraternal comes to us from the Latin *frater,* brother; *fraternitas,* fraternity. The Portuguese verb *fradejar* describes murmurings among friends, as friars are said to do, but also carries a sense of intrigue, entanglement, and gossip.

Fraternity is a polysemic philosophical concept, ranging from the specific quality of the relationship among siblings (brotherhood/sisterhood), to confraternization among people, countries, and races. Fraternity indicates a specific kind of union between people, a relational category (when reciprocity exists) and, at the limit, points to the broader idea of community – a group of people sharing common goods, values, habits.

Phratry, or *fratria* in Latin, is also in the dictionary: in ancient Greece, these were the subgroups of the Athenian tribes, in other words, a group of clans with similar characteristics. Similarity constructs difference. At an archetypal level we are released into the *logos* of the notions of similarity and difference. The notion of *fratria* thus returns us to the archetypal level of horizontally mutual relations: the brother/sister of the soul.

There are several sets of siblings and twins in the mythical stories that reach us through various traditions. The wealth of the images is all there and available in the myths, the fairy tales, the stories, and the clinic. Castor and Pollux, Helen and Clytemnestra, Amphion and Zeto, Remus and Romulus, Gilgamesh and Enkidu, Cain and Abel, Jacob and Esau, Hercules and Iphicles, Apollo and Hermes, Apollo and Artemis, Medea and Apsyrtus, the sisters of Psyche, Exú and Ogun, Horus and

---

19. http://www.merriam-webster.com/dictionary/fraternity (accessed 17 June 2016).

Seth, Isis and Osiris, Cosmas and Damian, the Ibejis, Iphige-
nia and Electra, Ariadne and Phaedra, Antigone and Ismene,
and the Greek mythological groups of sisters: the Danaids, the
Horae, the Graces, the Gorgons, the Furies, and the Fates. So
many patterns, so many faces: from cooperative twinship to
rivalry and fratricide. Certainly almost all the founding myths
in the Indo-European tradition involve stories of brothers.
Pairs of brothers appear in many of the stories about founding
cities: Amphion and Zeto founded Thebes; Castor and Pollux
founded Troy; Remus and Romulus founded Rome; and Cain
founded Enoch. Brothers and brotherhood found *polis*.

We must bear in mind, therefore, that the brother is the
political space *par excellence*—of course, when this space is not
in the authoritarian exception. Brotherhood is an anchor for
the notion of citizenship in classical Greece, for example. We
can recall that in Ancient Greece participation in citizenship
took place at three sequential levels. The first of these levels,
which founded the base for the rest, was exactly a *phratria,*
"brotherhood," the sum of the clans, that is, the families where
one was born, also known as *génos,* where blood ties determined belonging. Only after recognition by the *fratria* could
the Greeks enlist into a *demo,* a tribe (the *phylé*), to then reach
the third level, which is the level of activity in the city, the
polis itself, the sum of the clans, the *fratrias,* and the tribes.
The *fratria* was "an association founded on family relationships, alliances, and neighborhoods. Those who comprised one
call themselves "brothers... A *fratria* brings together rich and
poor, aristocrats and people of humble birth, without hierarchy. A *fratria* functions as a gathering structure."[20]

There are many "sibling mythologies." They attest the
fundamental importance of symmetrical relations. Here we

---

20. Giulia Sissa and Marcel Detienne, *Os Deuses Gregos* (São Paulo:
Companhia das Letras, 1990), 233.

are interested in their psychological value. Brother and sister stories are a part of all cultures and religious traditions, even though they tend to be given little attention. Greek mythology is a good example; many of its main gods and goddesses are siblings or twins, especially among the Olympians: Zeus and Hera, Apollo and Artemis, Apollo and Hermes. In their meaning and wisdom, they alternate stories symbolizing harmony and integration on one hand, and struggle, dispute, and conflict on the other.

In the Judeo-Christian tradition, Aaron and Moses are said to show a prototypical relationship between brothers and are an exceptional example of fraternal love. It is almost an exclusive exception. Their relationship contrasts with the other numerous stories of brother relations in the *Bible*. Cain and Abel is the very first one, a paradigmatic murder story; Isaac and Ishmael rivaled each other, and that rivalry extended through generations; Esau sold his birthright to his brother, Jacob, who thereby obtained the covenant blessing—the enmity that afterward subsisted between the twin brothers and the nations they founded is well known. Joseph and his brothers is another example of the biblical imagination of fraternal bonds. The rabbis dwell with special laudation on the brotherly sentiment that united Aaron and Moses. Aaron is the older brother and a prophet and served as his brother's spokesman because Moses has a speech impediment. When the latter was appointed ruler and Aaron high priest, neither betrayed any jealousy; instead, they rejoiced in one another's greatness. And of them it is written: "Behold how good and how pleasant [it is] for brethren to dwell together in unity!" (*Psalms* 133:1).

In other traditions, we also find divine healers, such as the important Asvin twins in Hindu mythology, who are similar to the Greek Dioscuri (Castor and Pollux): givers of honey, they rejuvenate the old and heal the sick, and appear mounted on their horses in the morning sky. In Yoruba mythology, the Ibejis, a set of boy and girl twins, the children of Oshun and Shango, protect children and "represent the renewal of the spirit, the birth of a new inner life";[21] they "preside over childhood and fraternity, duplicity, and the childish side of adults."[22] As divine children, they are connected and preside over the spring and initial stages of everything: a river head, the birth of human beings and animals, sprouts, buds of plants, the dawning of a new day.

In the field of classical mythology, however, the Spartan Dioscuri are closer to us. They represent the theme of "divine twins," which are relatively common in ancient Greece. Other examples of these pairs are Zethus and Amphion (Thebes), Parrhasius and Lycaste (Arcadia), and Idas and Lynceus (Messinia). Castor and Pollux (or Polydeuces), the most important, show us such a standard of cooperative twinship that their myth presents us with what may be the most advanced dimension of brotherly love. The eros that brought them together gives us the image of ideal friendship, or the ideal of friendship.

> As brothers, as an inseparable unit, the Dioscuri were widely worshipped throughout Greece...by committed male friends and lovers as embodying the ideal expression of deep male-male bonding. Their representation of brotherhood as a beautifully supportive but essentially extroverted, action-oriented relationship served as a model for all close male-male bonds.[23]

The word "Dioscuri" comes from the Greek *Diòs* and *koûroi*, the "youth/children of Zeus." Both are sons of the mortal Leda:

21. Zeca Ligiéro, *Iniciação ao Candomblé* (Rio de Janeiro: Record/ Nova Era, 1999), 105.
22. Reginaldo Prandi, *Mitologia dos Orixás* (São Paulo: Companhia das Letras, 2001), 22.
23. Downing, *Psyche's Sisters*, 56.

Pollux fathered by Zeus in the form of a swan, and Castor fathered by Tyndareus, Leda's husband. At their same birth, yet another pair of twins is born: their sisters Helen and Clytemnestra. They were simultaneously of both divine and mortal origin.

Many legends surround them, of birth and death, of battles as brave and powerful warriors, skillful and inseparable horsemen, of their adventures such as the hunt for the Calydonian boar and the expedition of the Argonauts. But the most important thing for us here is the tale that describes how one day the twins faced their enemy cousins, Idas and Lynceus. The mortal brother, Castor, was killed by Idas, while Pollux's father Zeus took him up to heaven. (Whenever the theme of twinship appears, often one brother must die to assure life to the other.) Pollux was extremely distraught at the loss of his brother and refused his immortality, which his father had recently revealed to him. Pollux did not want to be apart from his brother, who now as a mortal would remain in the kingdom of Hades for eternity. Pollux, who loved his brother more than his life, begged Zeus to return Castor to life. Such evidence of deep brotherly love moved Zeus, and Pollux received the following gift from his father: they would share immortality, with the twins spending one day among the gods on Mount Olympus, and one day in the tomb of heroes among the dead. And they appear in the skies as the constellation Gemini.

Another example in Greek mythology is the twins Amphion and Zethus. They were sons of Zeus and Antiope. Their mother had abandoned them, fleeing in shame because they were the product of a rape by Zeus (her husband was either King Nycteus of Thebes or the river god Asopus). Amphion became a great singer and musician after Hermes taught him to play and gave him a golden lyre; Zethus a hunter and herdsman. They punished King Lycus and Queen Dirce for cruel treatment of Antiope, their mother, whom they had treated as a slave. They built and fortified Thebes, huge blocks of stone forming themselves into walls at the sound of Amphion's lyre. Amphion married Niobe, and killed himself after the loss of his wife and children at the hands of Apollo and Artemis. Zethus married Aëdon. The brothers were buried in one grave.

In Roman mythology, Romulus and Remus were the twin sons of Rhea Silvia and Mars. They were, together with their mother, cast into the Tiber. The brothers were miraculously rescued by a she-wolf. The wolf reared the twins together with her cubs underneath a fig tree. After a few years they were found by the shepherd Faustulus, who took the brothers home and gave them to his wife Acca Larentia to raise. When they reached maturity they killed Amelius, the brother of their grandfather, and built a settlement on the Palatine Hill. During a quarrel where Remus mocked the height of the walls, Romulus slew Remus and became the sole ruler of the new Rome, which he had named after himself.

Twins have always stirred great interest, fascination, or even fear and horror among all mythologies and symbolic traditions, in all civilizations. Image of duality in similarity, they comprise the "state of ambivalence of the mythical universe," a "symbol of the very contingency of every human being divided in himself."[24] The foundation of many societies are linked to the appearance of twins, as the Indian populations of Alto Xingu, in Central Brazil, for whom the twins Sun and Moon have created humanity. Twinship brings us a special and radical image of horizontal symmetrical relationships, since—unlike any other human beings—they share the same uterus for seven to nine months, the same primordial shelter, and so they are born already companions.

---

24. Junito Brandão, *Mitologia grega*, 3 vols. (Rio de Janeiro: Vozes, 1998), 2: 79–80.

A tragic pattern of fraternal cooperation is radically presented to us in the myth of Procne and Philomela. Procne's husband Tereus rapes his sister-in-law, Philomela, and cuts out her
tongue so she can tell no one what happened. Torn apart by her
husband's infidelity, Procne learns of these events after receiv-
ing a tapestry woven by Philomela — abandoned in a cabin in the
woods — who chronicles her misfortune at the hands of Tereus,
and joins her sister for vengeance. Of all things, the cruelty she
found most appropriate was to serve her husband a banquet of
his own dismembered son, who she had killed for this purpose.
At the end of the meal, Tereus asked about the whereabouts of
their son and was horrified when Procne presented him with the
head of the child, Itys, on a platter as an explanation of the result
of the two sisters' furious conspiracy.

A tragic myth, it features the fraternal connection and the
compassion for the sisters' pain — obviously also driven by the
pain of marital betrayal — a connection that speaks even louder
than motherhood. The metaphor is simple: do not challenge
fraternal loyalty. [25]

---

25. The most complete rendering of the story of Philomela, Procne,
and Tereus can be found in Book VI of Ovid's *Metamorphoses*. This
story appears also in *The Waste Land* by T.S. Eliot, published in 1922,
where there is a very expressive scene for a reflection on psychotherapy and soul-making. It opens Part II of the poem, "A Game of
Chess." The scene describes in detail the sophisticated and claustro-
phobic atmosphere of the *boudoir* of a lady. With her is her husband,
or lover, silent. It is mainly the "portrait" of this lady who has something of a queen or princess, and the allusions of Eliot himself, in
the "Notes" which he added to the poem since its first edition, allude
nothing less than to the presence of Cleopatra — a modern Cleopatra, high urban class, nervous and scared, barren and forlorn. It is a
portrait of vanity. The whole environment is enveloped in perfumes,
aromas, light and shadow, glow jewelry, marble, chandeliers, figures. The superficiality of a world decorated and mute. There are, in

Another tragic pattern, one which is even more complex due to the multiple vectors of the various sibling relations it contains, appears in Sophocles's Theban plays, more precisely in the third of his tragedies about the Labdacids, *Antigone*. The drama begins at dawn on the day following the night when Antigone's twin brothers, Eteocles and Polyneices, die in battle at the hands of each other, disputing succession to their father Oedipus's throne of Thebes. Creon, Jocasta's brother and Antigone's uncle, took power, and his first act after ascending the throne was to forbid the burial of Polynices, under pain of death to anyone who tried. At the same time he ordered a hero's funeral for Eteocles, who died defending the city from his brother's attack. Antigone then decides to defy Creon and the city's laws and give her brother an honorable burial. Ismene, her sister, decides not to help.[26]

The play revolves around the discussion between natural law, which honors the laws of the gods and is championed by Antigone, and positive law, which honors the State's laws and

---

this setting of luxury and nobility, in its objects, references to various myths. Among them, and most significantly for the whole passage, Eliot takes us to the Philomela myth, suggested through a painting representing her metamorphosed into a nightingale, placed above the fireplace: "Above the antique mantel was displayed / As though a window gave upon the sylvan scene / The change of Philomel, by the barbarous king / So rudely forced." Philomela's myth, to which the poem refers directly in this scene, also testifies the subject of sexual brutality, rape, violation as well as the archetypal theme of death / rebirth, in her metamorphosis story. They are powerful images of pain and mangling. In an article published in the Brazilian Jungian journal *Cadernos Junguianos*, I addressed this scene, this myth, and its many psychological unfoldments: "Cores da sombra: o mito de Filomela e uma cena de Eliot," *Cadernos Junguianos* 3 (2007): 44–52.
26. Sophocles, *Theban Plays*, Brazilian translation from the Greek with notes and an introduction by Mário da Gama Kury (Rio de Janeiro: Jorge Zahar Editor, 1993).

is supported by Creon. But the dramatic backdrop against which all the action is justified is, in my view, Antigone's love and faithfulness to her brother Polynices. Antigone is a heroine of fraternity, deeply touched by the Sibling archetype:

> [She is] convinced that the kinship bond between siblings based on their common relationship to the mother, their origin in the same womb, transcends all other human and social obligations... [Antigone's] integrity as a human being is for her entirely dependent on her *being* a sister.[27]

In this single story, we have sibling rivalry and fratricide (Eteocles and Polyneices), fraternal loyalty (Antigone), dodging and desertion (Ismene), love, jealousy, power, envy, pride, solidarity, competition, and suicide — all surrounding the relationship between siblings. It is a true poetic compendium of emotions that shine brightly enough and also shadows these relationships. "There's no shame in revering those from the same womb," she tells her uncle, Creon. Antigone risks her life for her brother. Her logic is the logic of love. And she defends this logic in its radicalism:

> Never, I tell you,
> if I had been the mother of children
> or if my husband died, exposed and rotting —
> I'd never have taken this ordeal upon myself,
> never defied our people's will. What law,
> you ask, do I satisfy with what I say?
> A husband dead, there might have been another.
> A child by another too, if I had lost the first.

---

27. Downing, *Psyche's Sisters*, 69-70. And we must not forget that Eteocles and Polyneices, Oedipus's sons — who he curses before his death for having sent him into exile after the discovery of incest — are indeed his *brothers*, as are his *sisters* the daughters Antigone and Ismene.

But mother and father both lost in the halls of Death,
no brother could ever spring to light again.

For this law alone I held you first in honor ... [28]

Astrology, as a symbolic-mythological field, also help us psychologically realize and understand the enormous territory of the Other. It speaks of three Houses, or zodiacal zones, to understand our alterity experiences; by mapping them, astrology differentiates them. They are the *relationship houses*, symbolizing clearly three distinct levels of horizontal relations, which can be imagined, deepened, and experienced. Naturally, they mutually interconnect and inform each other. These are the houses of the element *air*, which has traditionally presided over the experiences of relationship. That probably means that the element air is the utmost symbol for relationships; but, on the other hand, it also means psychological experiences of distance and independence. Therefore, it balances the extreme poles of *separation* and *symbiosis*, which is the tension lying in the deepest base of all relationships.

Hence, astrology, when understood as a psychology of the archetypes, tells us how these relations are built: in the third house, corresponding to the sign of Gemini, which is the *brother's* house; in the seventh house, corresponding to the sign of Libra, the house of *partnership*; and in the eleventh house, corresponding to the sign of Aquarius, the house of *friendship*. From brother/sister, to partner, to friend: a horizontal route in the field of the Sibling archetype.

It is important to remember that these three planes, so to speak, are not arranged linearly in a direct sequence but, instead, in a circular fashion; in other words, they themselves require a nonhierarchical understanding. In this sense, astrology itself

---

28. Sophocles, *Antigone*, 995–1005. *The Three Theban Plays*, trans. Robert Fagles (New York: Penguin, 1984), 105–6.

offers the image and the example of a nonhierarchical understanding of archetypally influenced relationships, with its
essentially polycentric perspective, which is so well represented
on the astral chart itself, the astral wheel of the signs, plan-
ets, and aspects, where the forces or the symbols are arranged
equally and in equal slices around the circle of the zodiac.

Let us briefly observe how these levels work symbolically.
Most primordial is the third house, which rules the brother/
sister level, and will influence the development of our capacity to relate equilaterally at the level of an intimate partner,
and after that, of friends and groups. Hence, the third house
"symbolizes our primary encounters with others who shared
our environment, mainly the sibling/s, but also other neigh-
borhood friends and primary schoolmates."[29]

The seventh house, the house of the Partner, symbolizes
"the sphere of equality on an adult level, where we encounter others who feel familiar and complement what we sense is
missing in ourselves."[30] We find here mutuality and reciprocity relations, with those we can share and dream life projects,
for we feel committed and intimate. This includes the world of
marriage, the spouses, the family project, as well as the world
of business and professional accomplishments.

The eleventh house is the house of friendship, of the Friend,
and it "represents our encounter with equals in the community outside the familial setting, which includes the 'social others'—colleagues, associates, acquaintances, friends and professional equals. This is the house of groups, of organizations,
reminiscent of our first experience of an organization—the
family."[31] Here we can find brothers and sisters that we feel are

---

29. Clark, *The Sibling Constellation*, 162.
30. Ibid., 173.
31. Ibid., 177.

from the same spiritual tribe, what helps us deepen our values, ideas and projects.

We may understand perfectly that these levels are interconnected, for the symbolic system places them at the same affective horizon. Our experience as brothers and sisters determine and organize our capacity to make and keep friends. Positions, roles, ways of loving, unresolved hopes and desires, failures and resentments, shame and guilt brought by the fraternal original system, are taken to relationships with friends and coworkers, where they are constantly reactivated. This happens with the daily, most intimate bonds we have with our best friends; but also within the formality and obligations of professional organizations, of groups and community. Our brother (or our sister) is our first equal, and with him are formed the joys, sorrows, and wounds of symmetric relations, ruled by the Sibling archetype. In other words, our brothers and sisters come back to us in our friends. Our friends become our brothers/sisters. Thus, friendship relations are also a space for us to redeem wounds and conflicts of the fraternal system.

There are several numinous appearances of the Sibling archetype in the sphere of a culture's collective consciousness. *Fratria* as an archetype naturally goes beyond the individual sibling experience. A few obvious examples among so many allow us to perceive the emergence of the fraternal archetype not only in the classical myths of various civilizations, the astrological reasoning of the world, alchemy and mysticism in many traditions, but also in history, in Christianity (most heavily in St. Francis of Assisi), in the Buddha, in the ideals of the French Revolution, and in Gandhi.

One meaningful example, in education, would be the Escola da Ponte (Bridge School), an elementary school, located in Vila das Aves, Portugal, which was founded by the Portuguese educator José Francisco Pacheco in 1976 and radicalizes the principles of "democratic education"—an educational philosophy in which democracy and equality is both a goal and a method of instruction of children, started at the Summerhill School in Suffolk, England, in 1921. The school has no interior walls to separate students according to age or grade. They are grouped according to the area of interest to be searched, regardless of age. They are called to practice democracy within the school itself, as autonomous citizens. As in a direct democracy, they organize general meetings and discussions to solve discipline and other problems. Each student and educational adviser are responsible for one aspect of school operation. The student and even the teacher who break the rules, predetermined by themselves, are invited, before all, to reflect and decide on their behavior inside the school. Space is structured so that everyone can work with everyone. No student is a student of a teacher only, not a teacher teaches only a few students. The school works on a project logic, and is structured from the interactions between its members and the community. For me, this radical experience is clearly under the influence of the Sibling archetype.

But the example of St. Francis of Assisi, in the Western tradition, is paradigmatic. He goes beyond the vertical father-son relationship and lives the mystique of family ties in a way that is completely sensitive to the horizontal level, lives the brother/sister experience so radically it becomes possible to truly see everything and everyone as siblings: the trees, the mountains, the weeds, the animals, the waters, the stones, the rich, the poor, the children, the sick. With Francis, fraternity becomes universal: Brother Sun, Sister Moon. It is the gospel of fraternity, the spiritual novelty of fraternity that we gain from him, as indicated by Brazilian theologian Leonardo Boff in his many writings about St. Francis,[32] a fundamental model of his theology. St. Francis is at the root of an anthropology where the category of brother, soul brother, reveals a way of being that in the logic of the heart, in the logic of emotion, has a connection to all things and with all beings. With him, we can foresee a bright image of brotherly love, a more advanced model of the ideal of horizontality:

> There are no limits to his fraternity. And here is the sweetness, the courtesy, the tenderness in St. Francis. Because after all, what is the brother relationship? It is a relationship of love, of kindness, of emotion, of embraces, of affection. Siblings live this dimension.[33]

Finally, also in the body we can identify and appreciate the archetypal areas of brotherhood and fraternity, and also recognize its repression, its pathologizing. We can easily imagine that if the *lap* is the archetypal place of the mother, the space where affection takes place as a primordial image at the level of the womb (like shelter, protection, warmth, vessel, and a foundation for the soul, a base, a land, matter), then the essential archetypal *locus* for a sibling or friend will be the embrace, as also a primordial image, with the affection that encircles at the level of the chest, the heart chakra, *anahata*. Bosom buddy, brother, comrade: speaking of the bosom, from the chest, from the heart.

Of course, there's a heart in the belly, in the lap, a mother's heart, a heart in the womb that is free to love. But what about the heart in the breast that embraces, the chests that touch each

---

32. Leonardo Boff is a Brazilian theologian and writer, known for his active support for the rights of the poor and excluded. Boff entered the Franciscan Order in 1959. He became one of the best known supporters of the early liberation theology.

33. Jean-Yves Leloup and Leonardo Boff, *Terapeutas do deserto: de Fílon de Alexandria e Francisco de Assis a Graf Dürckheim* (Petrópolis: Vozes, 2002), 77.

other and open, diaphragms full and pointing upward, *ana-hata*? This is the heart of brotherhood, the body of fraternity, the psyche in the chest.

Transference

Now, the important clinical question of transference. I understand that the yearning, on the part of most patients who undergo analysis, for a transference of paternal/maternal character is established and even *reinforced* by the very methods of analysis which in themselves, as Hillman has taught us, perpetuate Oedipus and the vertical family, perpetuate the Mother and her concerns about origins and the emphasis on self-knowledge.[34] So these transferences—rather, these longings for love, these shortcomings of the soul, these portraits of helplessness and abandonment—are instigated or even produced by the method itself, by what we find when we enter into analytical relationships. Even if in a Jungian setting—where, in principle, the analytical partners are positioned *symmetrically* in space (though not in time), situated *into* the mutual position of dialog, and situated *for* the mutual position of dialog. Why, then, is sufficient importance not given in Jungian analysis to the perception of the appearance, the progress, and especially the *function* of fraternal transferences, of mutuality and equal reciprocity, in psychotherapy? If we remain in the method, we remain paternalistic and defended from the Sibling.

We find, in an important paper by Freud where he discusses the dynamics of the analytic relationship, the observation that transference is not necessarily linked only to the images of father and mother but can also arise from the *imago* of the brother ("The Dynamics of the Transference," 1912). Freud congratulates Jung for coining the term *imago*, which

---

34. James Hillman, "Oedipus Revisited," in *Mythic Figures, UE* 6.

sounds quite "suitable" to him, but he does not follow through with the reflection:

> As we should expect, this accumulation of libido will be attached to prototypes, bound up with one of the clichés already established in the mind of the person concerned, or, to put it in another way, the patient will weave the figure of the physician into one of the "series" already constructed in his mind. If the physician should be specially connected in this way with the father-imago (as Jung has happily named) it is quite in accordance with his actual relationship to the patient; but the transference is not bound to this prototype; it can also proceed from the mother- or brother-imago and so on.[35]

What Freud clearly indicates, and what we are trying to imagine, is that the analytic relationship may be under the powerful influence of the fraternal archetype in various ways, especially since this relationship can reflect the original positions of both the analyst and the patient in their original family constellations. Here we have, among others, the important issue of birth order, which we will examine later in Chapter 2. If the analyst is the oldest brother and the patient the youngest brother, for example, or even the opposite, or if one of them is an only child, we understand that certainly these positions may turn out to be determinant indeed, in a deeper unconscious sense, to model transference and countertransference. And at the limits, or in the light of the difficulties or ease found there, they can also determine the success or failure, the possibility or dramatic impossibility, of this (analytical) relationship.

---

35. Sigmund Freud, "The Dynamics of the Transference" (1912), in *Therapy and Technique,* ed. Philip Rieff, *The Collected Papers of Sigmund Freud* (New York: Collier Books, 1963), 107.

The fundamental clinical questions, in other words, are: how to make therapists aware of a connection based on this archetypal level, on the logic of fraternity? If I enter into analytical relationship at this level, what comprises it? What do I cause, what do I find out, what can I see, what changes in me and in the other? How many necessary and essentially fraternal transferences are abandoned, or even worse, are *not perceived* — or seen as resistance and therefore wasted — because of our own method? Questions of transference.

When family or familiarity is spoken of in the theory of depth psychology and the practice of analytical psychotherapy, it almost always refers to the drama of mother/father/children relationships. The bonds of siblings are never explored, as they could be in my opinion. And "family" is never imagined or considered in terms of the importance, whether structuring or destructuring, of these diverse fraternal ties. All of the plots that are part of sibling relationships stay in the background when we seek to profoundly understand behavior, relationships, emotions, reactions, pathology, diagnostics, language, dreams. Jung himself dedicated only fifteen lines, a single paragraph, in his memoirs to his only sister, without even mentioning her name, Gertrud, eventually stating that "she was always a stranger to me."[36] And he does not mention the two stillborn elder sisters, nor a brother, Paul, who immediately preceded him but lived only five days. What impact these sisters could have had on him and on his theory, with regard to the mystery of the feminine (or the mysterious and unknown feminine) — from the

---

36. C.G. Jung, *Memories, Dreams, Reflections,* ed. A. Jaffé; trans. R. and C. Winston (New York: Random House, 1961), 112: "...my sister, a delicate and rather sickly nature, in every respect different from me. She was as though born to live the life of a spinster, and she never married... I could imagine her spending her days in a Home for Gentlewomen, just as the only sister of my grandfather had done."

early experiments with his enigmatic cousin Helene Preiswerk through his most advanced formulations about the *anima* and the *soror mystica* in alchemy—is one of the arguments made in Brian Clark's book, *The Sibling Constellation.*

Horizontality

In an intriguing chapter of James Hillman's *Senex and Puer*,[37] he clearly sees *puer* phenomenology and psychology equated with ascending modes of consciousness, with transcendent and vertical directions in soul, with erection and erectability (archetypal and otherwise), and consequently also with ambition, competition, arrogance, and what psychology now calls "inflation"—as if *puer* consciousness ignored "the daily world and its incessant continuity." I want to call attention and concentrate for a moment on this "incessant continuity." Hillman goes on to show us that all those characteristics, if viewed from the *puer* perspective—and not from our ordinary ego perspective—reveal indeed a truly spirit phenomenology where transcendence becomes a way of transgression, and arrogance, ambition, and inflation could be understood as the emotions working toward "redemption, beauty, love, joy, justice, [and] honor"[38] in the world—aspects we so much lack in contemporary life. But ambition, arrogance, and even inflation take us up. What would take us forward?

To face and struggle with the "incessant continuity" of our daily world, the very idea of a *daily world,* would lead us away from the *puer* and closer to soul, moving us from verticality to horizontality: an anti-heroic move. And also an anti-erection move, for we would no longer go for erection *per se,*

---

37. James Hillman, "Notes on Verticality: Creation, Transcendence, Ambition, Erection, Inflation," in *Senex & Puer, UE* 3: 158–78.
38. Ibid., 175.

or archetypal erection, as with the *puer,* but for archetypal *penetration,* as with the *anima,* penetration in the horizontal plane—the world (and *not* beyond or away from it).

Erection is not a function of relationship, though magical or even miraculous it may be. "An erection serves less to relate lovers than to ride them heavenward in ecstasy. An arrow, not a bridge."[39] It lacks continuity, being utterly momentary, a moment in time. Maybe continuity is more a predicament of the *anima* than an aspect of the *senex. Anima* is what gets us involved with something, maintaining us in bonds, penetrating and being penetrated. The verticality of the spirit is intermittent, not incessant. It leaps: moments of insight, of vision, or the mystic moment. Soul and horizontality seem incessant, for soul is always with us, always there for us, being continuity itself, being our continuous and inexplicable complications with the world. What follows ascensionism, verticality, and erection is archetypal penetration into the world.

The "continuity" that does not cease *is* the world, the vale of soul-making. For the world of soul-making is a horizontal world, not ascendant, not transcendent: "Call the world if you please, 'The vale of Soul-making.' Then you will find out the use of the world…," are the famous lines by John Keats, which James Hillman used for his vision of soul work. This is the sphere of relationships and the interpenetration of all things, ideas, people, passions, pathologies, when we are horizontally aligned with the *anima* as that in us who then penetrates and is penetrated, who senses the world and is sensed by it. From this perspective, to be in the soul, *esse in anima,* is to be in a penetrative horizontal mode.

Hillman's work makes it easy for us to see how much we are caught into the conditions of the *puer/senex* archetype in

---

39. Ibid., 167.

our culture—conditioned to experience what is new and what is old, what is past and what is future, what is tradition and what is inspiration, everyday in our lives and in the world in ascensional terms, with vertical imaginings, ups and downs. Erections and depressions. If verticality is present in the *puer*, as Hillman so extensively shows us, it is as well relevant in the *senex*. Depression, melancholy, downwardness are important aspects of *senex* consciousness. "Saturnine" we call it, and feel its leaden weight. *Senex* consciousness involves us with depth, with the deepening of experiences, with weight, as if always in, so to speak, "downward ascensions": "The way up and the way down are one and the same" (Heraclitus, Fragment 60).

With the idea of an archetypal penetration in mind, we can now call upon the Sibling archetype and its impact on the world and on our relations to the world and to people, paradigmatic as it is of all horizontal symmetric styles of consciousness. It is primarily with brothers and sisters that we learn the difficult lessons of horizontality, continuity, symmetrical relationships, and soul-making. This means a deepening in the horizontal plane, toward the Other, the world and its events and complications. Depth—the great metaphorical direction in archetypal psychology—can also be imagined and experienced in a horizontal plane, with a penetrative fantasy. Soul can always deepen things also in horizontal connections.

So maybe what Jung recognized and understood as *anima* starts as a function of relationship in a horizontal level. If this is so, we can get back now to erection and penetration, where we just started—where everything starts—and say that if the *puer* is "up-and-down," *anima* is "in-and-out." In this perpendicular image we all need to perform the *puer-psyche* marriage, as Hillman has also suggested,[40] which for me means ask-

40. Hillman, *Senex & Puer*, UE 3: 85–89.

ing anybody who acts in the name of soul to find horizontal connections "between the *puer*'s drive upward and the soul's clouded, encumbering embrace." [41]

Horizontality: a mode of deepening.

---

41. Ibid., 84.

II. *The Psychopathology of Symmetrical Relations*

> And the Lord said unto Cain, Where is Abel thy
> brother? And he said, I know not: Am I my brother's
> keeper?
> —Genesis 4:9

Now I intend to present and discuss some aspects of the *shadow*
of horizontal symmetrical relations; in other words, the psychopathology of the relations between siblings, mostly, but also
logically extending into relationships with friends, companions, and comrades. How then to understand that we often live
these ties with rivalry, competition, suspicion, deception, distance, jealousy, revenge, disputes, betrayal, paranoia, fighting,
and even fratricide, authoritarianism and humiliation, conflict
or disinterest, crimes and punishments? How do we attain this
love, which is so often tinted with the sad colors of distance,
rupture, silence, or discord? Here the wounds are countless,
and care is urgent. The mythological background helps us to
better understand these situations in the larger archetypal
panorama of the Sibling archetype.

What, then, is the deeper meaning, and the broader emotional reverberations in other bonds, of the love and loyalty
between brothers and sisters, or, on the other hand, of fighting
and sibling rivalry, in the silence between siblings, brothers
and sisters who stop talking to each other? And what of the

difficulty, often impossibility, of maintaining close links to sustain closeness and difference, especially in the brother-sister pair? Why, as we have already mentioned, when one asks, this bond is difficult in most individual cases? How to overcome this difficulty and advance in these bonds? How does all this define and shape my soul? What does this have to do with my destiny? And how to free the horizons of the soul so it can finally fraternize?

Fraternal love

Understanding of *fratria* as a psychological experience can take place via three main routes: birth order, division of the sexes, and the number of children who comprise the sibling group. This allows assessment of the impact, characteristics, and scale that the Sibling archetype may have with relation to the character of a particular family constellation, as well as its influence on the lives of the individuals.

The impact of birth order deserves special attention. Later on in our lives we reproduce our rank among our siblings in our relationships, our marriages, and in our experiences with associations, partners, companions, and friends. Birth order, and each sibling's specific position in this order, is part of our destiny. As a strong influence on our way of life in adulthood, this order cannot be changed, we can only be made aware of it.

Although we may present them here in a more or less schematic manner, family arrangements typically occur within the following categories: the oldest sibling (the firstborn), the middle sibling (one or several), the youngest sibling (the baby), and the only child. From a psychological point of view, each of these positions clearly carries with it a way of relating to the others with unique characteristics, fantasies, problems, and aspirations.

Generally speaking, the oldest child is more likely to be heavily influenced by his or her parents' expectations for themselves as well as for their child. This leads to an anxiety that is normally present in older siblings, which can be perceived in their fantasies about success or in the pressure to be productive and to accomplish things. They stay more attached to the structures, traditions, and values of the family they were born into, unconsciously identifying more with their parents, and so issues of identity, self-esteem, and approval are always more prevalent. They tend to be more conservative.

Along with the arrival of new siblings comes the special and important issue of primogeniture (the right of succession belonging to the firstborn child). Various cultures throughout history have created a cult around the person and the position of the firstborn through habits, customs, mythology and religious traditions. The firstborn is often considered sacred. We all know the "case" of Esau and Jacob in *Genesis,* which recounts the importance and the archetypal implications of primogeniture. Although this practice has been abolished, the right to inherit all the "possessions" and "privileges" of the father can be seen as a metaphor of power, authority, and singularity, which are present in the unconscious psyche of the eldest son. It is a trigger that can arouse envy and greed among siblings.

Middle children obviously identify more with the position of mediator and negotiator. Younger than the oldest sibling, and older than the youngest sibling, the middle child can always see both sides of the issues, which makes it more difficult for middle children to take sides in situations of confrontation and conflict.

The youngest child, in turn, is the bearer of the new order, always identifying with the image of the revolutionary, with an eye to what is new and different. The youngest arrives in the family when all its members are already located in defined and structured positions, especially if the family group is large. The rules and the values have already been established and agreed upon, and the youngest sibling has a privileged angle that more naturally leads to questioning and a desire to experiment with other models. The youngest child can be welcoming, but confronts the values of the family in a more direct manner. As a result, the youngest child is more open to the realities outside the family circle, to novelties from beyond the household environment and its customs.

The only child does not have to share parental attention and also does not have the profound and decisive experience of having to deal with the powerful and ambivalent emotions that a sibling system provides. Consequently, an only child will tend to have a stronger connection with friends, cousins, and neighbors. In many different situations in life, these children have special difficulty being just one among many.

The experience of the Sibling archetype, and the role of the fraternal in our lives, is part of the mythologizing activity of the psyche: even without the literal experience of a blood tie, we search for a sibling and build fraternal stories. To greater or lesser degrees, we yearn for a sibling, and in searching for one we search for this intimacy, which is fundamental and made of all the unconditional security (or almost unconditional security) that only a link that we have not chosen but life has chosen for us can grant, a permanent bond of equality and likeness. It is also within (and because of) this security, which is peculiar to the fraternal bond, that hostility and aggression may be expressed, often in an unbridled manner. In contrast, in the parental relationship the expression of hostility is more threatening to the most primary feelings of identity, and therefore we avoid it, sometimes hiding or even taking our deepest affections elsewhere, making any deal we can. Clinical practice demonstrates this repeatedly. The relationship between siblings, especially same-sex siblings, becomes the most stressful, volatile, and ambivalent.

It is easy to notice that many firstborn children, at some point in the course of what we call childhood, ask for and fantasize about a "little brother." What is behind this longing? How can we understand it psychologically with more elaborate notions and values than just those that indicate the Shadow, or even the big question of the Other, the Mirror? Could it be the soul already asking for *horizontality,* the diverse depth contained in horizontality? Horizontality: a way to go deeper.

Another aspect of this search for the brother—which is the imperative of the archetype in becoming real and particular in our lives—is our need to belong to a group, to seek out the group, in various stages of our personal, social, and professional lives. We search for a group, a band to belong to, where we will feel like we fit in, finally identified—with those who are similar, who note our difference for us, our identity, in that yearning for the other who is like me: parity.

Freud and Jung stopped there in their approaches to the subject. Freud spoke of sibling rivalry and explored the feelings of competition between siblings when another family member appears. And Jung mentioned on several occasions in his work only the "motive of the two hostile brothers" as an archetypal reality inherent to the psyche. Both remain within this unique aspect of the phenomenology of the Sibling archetype: rivalry, competition, hostility.

What we call depth psychology, however, emerged and established itself in the Eurocentric environment of a patriarchal culture, where white male authority and domination used to go unquestioned. Psychoanalysis then developed in the twentieth century with an almost exclusive focus on the asymmetrical hierarchy structures of the family (in other words, parental relations), largely ignoring the impact of sibling relations and their continuing influence throughout life, remaining only in the understanding and elaboration of the powerful mark that parents leave on our psyche.

In this context, we habitually refer to Sigmund Freud and C.G. Jung. However, we forget that there was a third founder of depth psychology, a third "brother," whose theories were very familiar to Jung (who himself recommended the works of this third brother),[1] and who Freud dismissed as "hardly psychological": Alfred Adler. His important contribution speaks mainly of human inferiority, of the "inferiority complex," of a sense of imperfection, namely what leaves us feeling inferior and broken—the weak point as the soul's place of least resistance. It was an important issue for psychotherapy, one that Jung formulated later as the *shadow*, albeit with different meanings.

Adler was the first (and the only one of the three) to talk about the powerful influence of the siblings in the construction of character and lifestyle of each personality. Prior to 1918, he was mainly concerned with the individual's position in the birth order, which has a major importance in his theory. Adler's emphasis on birth order, rather than, say, gender, is a way to desexualize either Freud's or Jung's theories; but, most important to the Sibling archetype, it is a way of considering verticality *within* the experience of horizontality.

However, another of his themes, which is also very significant in the context of our discussion, interests us more and indicates the direction I wish to pursue: what Adler called *Gemeinschaftsgefühl*, the sense of community (as an expanded

---

1. "No one who is interested in 'psychoanalysis' and who wants to get anything like an adequate survey of the whole field of modern psychiatry should fail to study the writings of Adler. He will find them extremely stimulating, and in addition he will make the valuable discovery that exactly the same case of neurosis can be explained in an equally convincing way from the standpoint of Freud or of Adler, despite the fact that the two methods of explanation seem diametrically opposed to one another" (Jung, *Freud and Psychoanalysis*, CW 4: 756).

sense of identity), or "fellow feeling," which he considered "the only realistic goal of psychotherapy."[2] James Hillman, in one of the rare trials of Jungian character that sought to recover the importance of Adlerian psychology for the practice of analytical psychotherapy, advanced an understanding of this sense of community, or "social interest," as he puts it, until attaining the idea of the soul of the world—as that movement that goes "from *my* soul to *the* soul, from *my* anima to *anima mundi*, from subjective feelings to objective world ensouled."[3] It seems to me an important broadening of the concept of "psychic reality" that launches us into community, into communion with all things.

Nevertheless, the importance of the complex notion of *Gemeinschaftsgefühl* above all lies in the fact that it is the only notion in the field of depth psychology to draw attention to symmetrical relations, and accordingly to move toward the sibling. It is a notion that we can say is based on the Sibling archetype. "For Adler, neurosis is an expression of the failure to recognize the inner meaning of sibling experience; the neurotic is trapped in the fantasy of being the only child, in the illusion of isolation."[4] According to this notion, the psyche needs to spread horizontally and *yearns for symmetry*. The soul longs for community:

> ...it wants to live with reason in a world that reflects cosmic meaning, then, now and forever, where the soul as the potential of this order strives with purpose and gives meaning to each act, as if each act "contributed" to life, moving it toward communal and cosmic perfection.[5]

---

2. James Hillman, *Healing Fiction* (Putnam, Conn.: Spring Publications, 2009), 124.

3. Ibid., 125.

4. Christine Downing, *Psyche's Sisters: Re-Imagining the Meaning of Sisterhood* (New Orleans: SpringJournal Books, 2007), 113.

5. Hillman, *Healing Fiction*, 107–8.

The soul seeks a deep experience of community, as one of its strongest needs. Loneliness—which has nothing to do with, on the one hand, the number of people around us or in our lives, and, on the other, with the encounters that one may have with oneself, or even with the painful awareness of our lonely road—is the great wound and the large complaint that emerges from oblivion and from neglect or even from the misrepresentation and perversion of this need. And so, one after another, we move from churches to organizations to institutions to groups and to neighborhoods, in despair and not with a perspective of soul.

Adler was not well understood, and remains partly forgotten. His precious concept of *Gemeinschaftsgefühl* was confused with social commitment and political work (in its various aspects, from social work to fundamentalist action), with the same literalism that reduced psychology to Freud's interest in sexuality, or Jung's interest in religion, also taking them literally—a point that has already been thoroughly explored by Hillman.[6] Instead of sex, religion, or community, the point is the *psyche* in these experiences, the soul of these experiences, or what the soul is communicating through these experiences.

What the psychological backing for this negligence with respect to the figure of Adler means is what most interests me here. To do so, before going further, it will be important to quickly recap some biographical information about the sibling constellations of these men who are acting as our fathers, so that we can better understand our theme. Freud and Jung were the oldest children in their families, they were the first born. Adler, on the other hand, was the second child after an older brother (by the name of Sigmund!). Freud, in a complex family constellation, had two much older half-brothers from his father's

---

6. "What does the Soul Want? Adler's Imagination of Inferiority," in ibid., 83–129.

first marriage (at the time of Freud's birth, his father was already a grandfather), and five younger sisters from his father's second marriage (to Freud's own mother). Jung, in turn, had only one surviving sister, and two sisters had been stillborn before him. We must also remember here that this triumvirate of founders, Freud, Adler, and Jung, each had a brother who died early, leaving them without rivals, so to speak. None of them, however, wrote a single line concerning the emotional impact of losing a brother or about the psychology of the concrete brother-sister relationship. Jung spoke of the *soror mystica* in alchemy, and the symbolic relationship between the adept and this figure as an image of *coniunctio,* and in doing so remained at the exclusively archetypal level of this topic. His only sister, Johanna Gertrud, who was nine years younger, is rarely mentioned in Jung's major biographies; he was known to refer to this relationship only rarely, and always with some awkwardness. Brian Clark speculates whether there had not been an "unconscious defense" on the part of the fathers of depth psychology against the symmetrical relations of brotherhood/sisterhood. That is, a defense of depth psychology itself, in which these relationships were unconsciously felt to be so problematic that the only recourse was to *not validate them*:

> The fathers of psychoanalysis, Sigmund Freud, Alfred Adler and Carl Jung, were also colleagues. Their fraternal relationship was fractured by rivalries as each one brought his personal sibling experiences to his collegial relationships... Their lack of focus on the sphere of siblings may have been an unconscious defense to maintain the seat of authority. [7]

---

7. Brian Clark, *The Sibling Constellation: The Astrology and Psychology of Sisters and Brothers* (Arkana: Penguin Books, 1999), 7–8.

We might speculate something like a "fraternal complex." This alone already points to the psychopathology of sibling relations. The constant conflicts and divisions and splits in the field of depth psychology might also be better understood from this historical/psychological background.

The field of comparative mythology, folklore, literature, religion, and folk tales, as I have already mentioned, has a dazzling array of stories and legends that cast light on the many sides of these ties and their inherent difficulties. However, I believe that for psychology and culture the true importance of symmetrical, horizontal relationships can only emerge and make us more aware of their influence when the hierarchical focus on asymmetrical parental relations (which, though loving, will always hide the specter of power and domination) has been abandoned. Only when the lenses of hierarchy have lost their predominant place in our view of the world and of ourselves, and in a linear view of the psyche, can a renewed sensitivity to equality actually step onto the stage. It is all we need. For I understand it is the difficult experience of equality and symmetry which is at the heart of the Sibling archetype, both in our personal lives and on the broader stage of culture and politics.

Various pairs of brothers have come down through the mythical stories of diverse traditions: Castor and Pollux, Romulus and Remus, Gilgamesh and Enkidu, Cain and Abel, Apollo and Hermes, Isis and Osiris, to again mention just a few of the most representative. So many patterns: each one tells a piece of the larger story of symmetry in human relations.

Being Wounded by a Sibling: Cain and Abel

In order to understand more deeply the question of brotherly/ sisterly love and its importance to soul-making, we should now turn to some aspects of its psychopathology, its suffering. From an archetypal point of view, we can see that the most fundamental psychological factors between siblings are the processes of negotiation, cooperation, and competition. Love between siblings runs through these processes. And it is through them that we can get a better glimpse of the shadow of symmetrical relations, or more importantly, symmetrical relations as pathology in the individual and in the culture. Here, there are two levels that can be glimpsed simultaneously: on the one hand, the wounds that are typical of brother/sister relations, in the various patterns that comprise a psychopathology of symmetrical relationships; and, on the other hand, brotherhood/sisterhood relations themselves as a wound, in other words, the shadow in which these relationships are found in the broader field of history and culture.[8]

Being wounded by a sibling, or feeling wounded by a sibling, involves hostility, aggression, and eros. The emotions involved are predominantly jealousy, envy, and hatred. But additionally, *the sibling is the wound,* an area in the soul that is clearly off-limits according to the patriarchy of the Judeo-Christian mythological tradition. Rivalry and envy, jealousy and contention are part of the fraternal constellation because they are deeply rooted in our cultural and religious tradition. The story of Cain and Abel is the paradigm of this wound. Let's take a look at how this particular story speaks to us of this wound.

We recall that Castor and Pollux, for instance, present an older polytheistic tradition of cooperation and fraternal love; Cain and Abel, in our Judeo-Christian monotheistic tradition, represent a pattern of brotherly rivalry and hostility. Castor

---

8. A detail: if we look at the civil ephemera, in Brazil and in various other countries we see the curious fact that we celebrate Mother's Day, Father's Day (even Children's Day and Lovers' Day in Brazil), but no Brother's Day appears on any official calendar. This is certainly part of the block against this topic.

and Pollux are *beneficent*: they are healers; they protect men from danger and save sailors. They work together in affinity.[9] Cain and Abel, on the other hand, antagonize each other, compete and disagree, acting separately, as in so many other myths of heroes and gods who are brothers. The two stories are very different: two aspects of the same bond; two faces of the same eros.

According to the story in Genesis 4, right at the very beginning of the first book of the Bible and well known to all, Cain and Abel are brothers vying for the attention and love of their father. Their competition turns into a fight that ends in the first murder in Judeo-Christian mythical history. And murder is the first crime, at the beginning of the moral perversion of man. In other words, this history (our history) begins precisely with a *murder*. This is the point I wish to emphasize. What is at stake is their father's favor: Cain, a settled farmer, offers him the fruits of his labor (fruits and grains), while Abel, the younger son and a shepherd, offers the best of his livestock (a bloody sacrifice of a sheep). Abel was a keeper of sheep; Cain, a tiller of the ground. This dispute enters into the larger archetypal conflict between an agrarian fantasy and a nomadic fantasy, between farmer and shepherd, between attachment to the land and animal mobility. *Shepherd, farmer,* and — I would add — *hunter* are three basic archetypes in the Western psychological tradition. In our interior life, and in our reactions to the world, we always find ourselves among them: we are either characterized and behave as shepherds or as farmers — or hunters.[10]

---

9. "The twin-ship of Castor and Pollux differs from other myths of twins in that their story aspires towards the achievement of affinity" (Clark, *The Sibling Constellation*, 118).

10. In another significant pair of hostile biblical brothers, Jacob is a shepherd, and Esau a hunter.

As Leon Kass suggests,

> Farming requires intellectual sophistication and psychic discipline: wit is necessary to foresee the possibility of bread from grain, to develop tools, to protect crops; self-control—indeed, a massive change in the psychodynamics of need and satisfaction—is needed before anyone will work today so that he might eat months later... The shepherd, in contrast, lives a simple and by and large artless life. His work is mild and gentle; his rule requires no violence. The sheep graze as they roam and produce wool and milk out of their own substance, the shepherd contributing nothing but also harming nothing.[11]

These also reflect different levels of relationship with Mother Earth, as clarified by Mircea Eliade:

> It is obvious, for example, that the symbolisms and cults of Mother Earth, of human and agricultural fertility...could not develop and constitute a complex religious system except through the discovery of agriculture; it is equally obvious that a pre-agricultural society, devoted to hunting, could not feel the sacrality of Mother Earth in the same way or with the same intensity... Nevertheless, between the nomadic hunters and the sedentary cultivators there is a similarity in behavior that seems to us infinitely more important than their differences: *both live in a sacralized cosmos,* both share in a cosmic sacrality manifested equally in the animal world and in the vegetable world.[12]

---

11. Leon R. Kass, "Farmers, Founders, and Fratricide: The Story of Cain and Abel," http://www.firstthings.com/issue/1996/04/april (accessed 20 November 2015).

12. Mircea Eliade, *The Sacred and the Profance: The Nature of Religion*, trans. Willard R. Trask (Orlando: Harcourt, Inc., 1959), 17. The vocation of these two men, these first two brothers—although there is a

The Father accepts Abel's gift, thereby indicating the superiority of animal sacrifices over vegetable sacrifices.[13] In a fit of jealous rage, Cain slits his brother Abel's throat with a sharp stone. Cain kills his only brother and thus kills the possibility of brotherhood, the possibility of symmetry.[14] So Cain becomes the first murderer in history, the "inventor" of homicide, the revealer of death; Abel, the first man to die, is considered by some to be the first martyr. The Hebrew God then decides that Cain can no longer work the land and must instead become an eternal fugitive, doomed to wander east of Eden to the land of exile, the Nod desert, where eventually he builds a city, Enoch. The first child of the first couple receives a severe punishment for his crime. Here, things are all very inaugural: we are in *Genesis*. And he receives a mark, a sign on the forehead between his eyes, so that from then on he can be recognized by everyone, especially so that he cannot be killed, following the law of vengeance. About this mark, James Hillman has something to say regarding our relations with the psychic world and dreams:

> Each morning we repeat our Western history, slaying our brother, the dream, by killing its images with interpretative concepts that explain the dream to the ego. Ego, over black coffee (a ritual of sympathetic magic), chases the shadows of the night and reinforces his dominion. No one sees the mark of Cain where his third eye could be.[15]

---

third brother, Seth (Genesis 4:25)—is to be brothers and to be different: in character, in their activities, in their relation to Mother Earth, and in relation to the Father.

13. The text itself does not tell us why Abel's offering of the firstlings of his flock is more palatable to the Lord than Cain's gift of fruit from the soil.

14. This homicide is the rupture of human fraternity. And in this sense, every homicide is a fratricide.

15. James Hillman, *The Dream and the Underworld* (New York: Harper

Especially with regard to the Sibling archetype, our mythological and cultural tradition begins with a story of dispute, rivalry, and jealousy between brothers that leads to fratricide and exile. The wound is very deep. Consider this metaphor: exile. From the beginning, the myth places sibling relations into an environment of horror, death, and failure. This leads to exile. In a monocentric culture where the Father is the foremost power, there is no place for symmetrical relations.[16] The emotions of envy and jealousy, which are always so corrosive and pathologized, are paradigmatically included in this tale.[17] We need to enter the fantasy of these emotions to more deeply understand the primal wounds and the shadow of symmetrical relations. Although they often capture our souls in a very similar and sometimes confusing manner, envy, and jealousy are quite different emotions: one is a desire for what someone has, while with the other we fear that someone else will take what we have and is ours. "Envy," from the Latin *invidere,* means "to look inside" with malice, to cast an evil eye upon; "jealousy," from the Latin *zelosus* and the Greek *zelos,* full of zeal, of fervor, alludes to a more complex emotional state, when we fear loosing something.

& Row, 1979), 116.

16. In a very different story, the brothers Hermes and Apollo have to come to terms with each other by order of Father Zeus. Cain and Abel quarrel because of the Father, YHWH. Here are two quite different patterns of relationship with the Father, two models of authority.

17. The history of privilege in the Hebrew Bible begins with Adam and Eve. Adam has a privileged position in relation to Eve, and privileged positions, along with focus on "elected ones," are central to this book. Privileged positions constellate envy. All along we have the motive of the chosen one, the elected one, occupying a fundamental archetypal position. Many important passages thus place hierarchy as measure of all relationships, and so we have a myth that depends on the instance of hierarchy, or asymmetry, to narrate itself.

Envy occurs in the context of a relationship involving two persons or two sides, while jealousy needs a triangle. Envy is two-dimensional; jealousy, three-dimensional. The imagination of envy functions in desire, while in jealousy it is fear. For the heart, the effect is the same: devastating and shameful. It is a big shadow: envy became one of the seven deadly sins, while jealousy is a humiliation. Envy involves power, while jealousy involves love. Envy is that madness occurring when we compare ourselves with others and stay away from ourselves, as understood by Rafael López-Pedraza. But we never wonder where those emotions want to take us.

Jealousy and envy arise in rivalry, which in turn is the shadow of intimacy and cooperation; it directly harms our capacity to *familiarize* ourselves, to get familiar with something, and pushes us into "exile." With our siblings we learn to divide and to share, we learn horizontal nonhierarchical relations, so our sensitivity to equality starts here. Sibling rivalry, this affront to equality, deeply affects our subsequent ability to share, to belong, and to be part of groups and neighborly relations. It therefore affects the amplitude of the soul in the horizontal world. In other words, it affects our experience of community, the feeling for our fellows, *Gemeinschaftsgefühl.*

But on the other hand, it is through this shadow that we are initiated into the distinctions between friend and enemy, the more advanced and sharp distinctions we need to make between companions and adversaries, between familiar and strange, between singularity and otherness. A sibling is both different and same *at the same time,* and it is through this paradox that the soul finds its way in the horizontality of the world. My point is: the Sibling is the archetypal basis for constructing the Other, and stands now as a possibility for recreating an idea and a sense of community within the "new orders" of the contemporary West.

However, if we understand these processes as archetypically determined, it is because we can see in them the presence of a divine person. This person, I believe, is Hermes. Anyone familiar with López-Pedraza's book on Hermes[18] can certainly benefit immensely from its investigation into the psychology of this god and his precious insights into the archetypal nature of the hermetic constellations.[19] Therein, López-Pedraza speaks of the margins where the god of commerce and trade is mythologically found. This plays precisely to our topic. Through the archetypal presence of Hermes—the "non-authoritarian God" (López-Pedraza), and remember, the god of roads and paths, a definer—the play between siblings starts us learning about connection, commerce, trade, about dividing and sharing, winning and losing, as well as about separation, deception, betrayal, duality, and polarity. The presence of Hermes always imposes a limit and a duplicity, since he is found on the borders and governs frontiers: "A series of epithets honor Hermes as god of ways and entries."[20] Hermes's borderline "implies a symmetry in relationship," as stated by López-Pedraza.[21]

In the territory of siblings, of twins, of symmetrical relations, we are always on a border or at a limit, always on the edges, having to deal more sharply with separations and identifications: on the edge between what I am and what I am not, where what I am and what I am not are *symmetrically* related.

---

18. Rafael López-Pedraza, *Hermes and His Children* (Zurich: Spring Publications, 1977).
19. See also Karl Kerényi, *Hermes: Guide of Souls* (Putnam, Conn.: Spring Publications, 2008).
20. Walter F. Otto, *The Homeric Gods: The Spiritual Significance of Greek Religion,* trans. Moses Hadas (Boston: Beacon Press, 1964), 114.
21. López-Pedraza, *Hermes,* 15.

(But here, take heed, we are not exactly dealing with the problem of the *shadow*, in the Jungian sense, because the shadow, it is worth remembering, is always *also* what I am.)

Demarcating territory is an essential part of the sibling experience. So we are, in a broader sense, under the reign of Hermes/Mercury, whose very nature is borderline. It is in this way that we can better understand the participation and influence of this god in all symmetrical relations.

In his book, López-Pedraza makes a long journey through Hermes's relationship with his brother Apollo, which is so fundamental to understanding Hermes's epiphany. With him we learn that there is more soul in the distance filled with connection, in that "true distance" López-Pedraza speaks of, than in that contact that only serves to blur the boundaries and differences, erasing real connection:

> The relationship between the two brothers improves substantially when Hermes promises "he would never steal anything of all the Far-shooter possessed and would never go near his strong house." With this promise there is a delineation of their two fields which, of course, soothes Apollo and he is ready to love Hermes above all others. It is the defining the limits of their two fields of action, marking the boundaries, that brings about a movement into love, eros, between the two brothers. A true distance has been made.[22]

Similarity in difference reveals, in this sense, an advanced level of hermetic consciousness. This is, I wish to believe, an important topic and the hardest lesson of fraternal relations.

Brothers and sisters, after all, are those who bring us the deepest sense of *duality*, and in this way it is an initiation: "an awareness that individuality is not essentially unity but

---

22. Ibid., 50.

a doubleness, even a duplicity, and our being is metaphorical, always on two levels at once."[23]

James Hillman understands this point (which is also the archetypal theme of the Double):[24]

> Only this twofold truth, *gloria duplex,* can offer protection against shipwreck by teaching us to avoid foundering upon the great monolithic rocks of literal realities... Wherever one is, there is always an "other" by means of whom we reflect existence and because of whom we are always "more," "other," and "beyond" what is here-and-now.[25]

Consciousness of duality is, therefore, at the heart of the experience the Sibling archetype. This is a primordial experience in this double field, the field of the Other (within ourselves and in the external reality). One of the gods of Yoruba (African) mythology, for example, is an *orisha* who is permanently doubled: the Ibejis. The Ibejis respect the basic principle of duality and are known to be protector of twins.

Jung, in his essay "Concerning Rebirth," from 1950, also mentions consciousness of duality as important in individuation, and in natural processes of transformation—and uses the image of the "inner friend of the soul" to refer to the other being in ourselves to which Nature wants to connect us. But still he brings the mythological image of Castor and Pollux, that is, the imagination of twinship, of brother's love:

---

23. Hillman, *Senex & Puer, UE* 3: 189.
24. The Double has little to do with the Sibling archetype per se, that is, the fraternal as a source of the feeling and the experience of horizontality and equal relatedness. The Double ultimately expresses the need to be connected to oneself, to an inner immortal soul—who then might present itself in dreams and fantasies as an inner same-sex sibling.
25. Ibid., 189.

> We are that pair of Dioscuri, one of whom is mor-
> tal and the other immortal, and who, though always
> together can never be made completely one. The
> transformation processes strive to approximate them
> to one another, but our consciousness is aware of
> resistances, because the other person seems strange
> and uncanny, and because we cannot get accustomed
> to the idea that we are not absolute masters in our own
> house. We should prefer to be always "I" and nothing
> else. But we are confronted with that inner friend or
> foe, and whether he is our friend or foe depends on
> ourselves. [26]

The psychopathology of the relations of this archetype teaches us that *failure* to recognize the duality that is fundamental and inherent to all human existence takes us directly to what Jung later identified as one-sidedness. One-sidedness is the specific Jungian definition of neurosis. [27] This failure later will also be better formulated within the framework of archetypal psychology as the fall of consciousness into the literal perspective of all things, in other words, the "loss of metaphor" or of the metaphorical double meaning of all events: the loss of duality. And here lies the more primary and insidious psychological error, the one that yanks us away from a soul consciousness.

Well, it is mainly this sense of duplicity that we lose when sibling relations are damaged, which of course casts a dark shadow over the entire topic of equality.

And it is exactly here, in this dark shadow, that we find our topic: when repressed, brotherhood/sisterhood, equality and symmetry, can only lead to authoritarianism, power

---

26. *CW* 9.1: 235.
27. *CW* 16: 257: "The neurosis is as a rule a pathological, one-sided development of the personality, the imperceptible beginnings of which can be traced back almost indefinitely into the earliest years of childhood."

relationships, domination and oppression, dependency, child-ishness—in both the personal as well as the collective spheres. It is with the archetypal Sibling that we construct in our souls the experience and meaning of equality and symmetry, which are so important to success or failure in the various significant relationships we establish during our lives. And it is also with him/her that we break these experiences.

The experience of the Sibling archetype launches us into a polycentric field, and this complicates us, since it points to a horizontal network of relationships. The experience of the Sibling archetype makes things more complex for us.

As a result, opposition and complementarity, separation and identification by themselves constellate the "fraternal problem": brothers and sisters are the persons who were born of the same womb and indicate my double, my duplicity. Here, more than any other place, we are on the path to the paradox, the hermetic road of contradiction and ambiguity: a meeting place, a place to meet the others. The Sibling archetype, more than anything, places us facing the *dynamics of difference,* a theme that is timely around the world. It indicates the always unsettling experience of Otherness.

III. *Siblings and the Reconstituted Family*

One form of family diversity that moves away from traditional notions is the stepfamily, now more commonly known as the "reconstituted family." A reconstituted family, or blended family, is the sociological term for the joining of two adults via marriage, cohabitation, or civil partnership, who have had previous relationships and children from them. All the members come together as one unit forming a new family. The reconstituted family represents an important field and a significant challenge in the contemporary psychotherapeutic clinic.

Let me return one last time to a passage from the quote by James Hillman that started all these reflections on the fraternal archetype, now in order to make some comments on the situation of the siblings with regard to the reconstituted family, their fantasies, and their problems. In the passage, Hillman initially points to the topic of the *reconstitution* of the family. Still from that same note from *The Myth of Analysis* that I already quoted in search of new insights, let us recall some of his words:

> The reconstitution of the family can be based on nei-
> ther the former metaphor of parent and child nor the
> new one of a democratic "functional" family. To rec-
> reate family in our generation, eros and psyche must
> have the possibility of meeting in the home... [1]

This perspective rests not upon hierarchical relationships of parents and children and the issues of early childhood, author-ity, and rebellion but in symmetrical relationships, such as be-tween siblings.

According to the inspiration of those words, the yearning that eros and psyche can meet, or meet again, in a situation of symmetry precedes the reconstitution of the family. This would be a more *psychological* paradigm (in contrast to socio-logical or even legal paradigms) for the reconstitution of the family itself. It has the character of a true commitment. And it brings with it the echo of the Sibling archetype. New connec-tions and new arrangements in the family context cannot take place without it being present at the same time.

To recreate the family in our lives, eros and psyche should be able to meet again in the home. In the formation of a new family, with the advent of new members (new fathers or new mothers, and new brothers and sisters who existed before or sprang from this new union), and with the more or less prob-lematic relations between former spouses, what is at stake is the search for reconstitution of a significant and creative eros in the lives of those people who seek to restore these estab-lished links we call "family." Just this *eros,* which will have no reality if it is far from an experience full of *soul,* will be able to sustain the difficulties and challenges of the task, and even the full success of a reconstruction. On the contrary, the effort is

---

1. James Hillman, *The Myth of Analysis: Three Essays in Archetypal Psy-chology* (New York: Harper & Row, 1978), 57n56.

bureaucratic, and will only be within the comfortable/uncomfortable sphere of the *persona,* and it will naturally prove to be empty.

Our modern experience of "family" derives from a Latin idea. We have already mentioned that this idea refers to the home, and everything that belongs to it or is found within it, such as movable and immovable property, furniture and objects, inhabitants and their guests, animals and things, heritage and ancestry, and the spirits of this ancestry. The reconstitution of the family follows this same unconscious fantasy, and reinforces the same idea: what goes into the "home" in a more or less permanent character, becomes *family.*

Note, again, an intense play on the words *family* and *familiar.* Here this is a play between similarity and difference, which establishes possible or impossible relationships between "equal" and "other." This is, in my view, the archetypical essential and deepest sense of the idea of family in the human experience. Of course, this meaning comes up against the archetype of horizontality, the fraternal archetype and its challenges, as I have been wanting to demonstrate.

But an important distinction must be made between the notions of reconstituted family and recomposed family. Reconstitution is a much more complex process than simple recomposition. Heart and soul are driven to this process. The decomposition of an old arrangement, a former love that is no more, follows a fantasy and a yearning that is deep and full of complications that is better described by the term *reconstitution.* A reconstitution is a reconstruction.

In the reconstituted family we understand, for example, that the children are being constructed/constituted, and the parents are being reconstructed/reconstituted. This puts two (or more) generational times into the same scenario, and the relationships between these psychological times is the source of and the stage for significant misunderstanding as well as psychopathology.

As we know and live it today, the experience of family primarily occurs along three main lines: the marital relations of the parent; the parents' relationships with their children; and finally, relations between the siblings. In these fields, we experience the constant interconnections, both composed and complex (and also so often, problematic), between asymmetrical relations and symmetrical relations. Maternalism and paternalism, on the one hand, and fraternity on the other continuously and mutually influence each other, and in some cases even get confused. The new orders of the contemporary family indicate a large amount of experimentation in these relations, experiments that are not always very successful. Parents-siblings, children-parents, siblings-parents: traditional vectors of family relationships rearrange themselves since they no longer fit into the old models. The Aquarian *aeon* requires emotional efforts that have yet to be developed.

From the point of view of symmetrical relationships, the experience of a reconstituted family represents the opportunity to also broaden the notion of *fratria*. The idea and the experience of an extended family that the reconstituted family brings leads us to also recognize, from the point of view of the siblings, the experience of an expanded *fratria*. Only from an expanded notion of *fratria* can we understand and experience then a "reconstituted *fratria*." In turn, an expanded *fratria* places us again before the difficult challenges of horizontality, of sharing, of dividing, of negotiating, in a manner that is often more dramatic, since it brings along with it the emergence onto the scene of new brothers and sisters, with whom we have to deal at this level.

It also brings the experience of situations that create new models of rivalry and/or affinity: the very discovery of new and unexpected (and sometimes unwanted) affinities; the development of new affective arrangements, where "new" brothers or sisters are often closer than the biological ones. The very bond of brotherhood/sisterhood, in the previous experience that we may have had with *fratria*—which is so important, as we have seen, to the constitution of the individual and their relations—if it was broken, blocked, or damaged in the family of origin, it now has an opportunity to be *reconstituted*, re-engineered, rebuilt. On the other hand, situations of conflict can be more frequent, and almost always reflect the difficult division of parental affections. And this is where negotiations, living arrangements and division of time, attention and money come into play.

In the expanded *fratria*, figures that appear in this scenario are: the "false sibling," or the children that come along with the new spouse, and the "half-brother/sister," the child of the new couple. From the point of view of the new couple, these are the "stepchildren."

Thus, from the perspective of the siblings, or from the relationships of horizontality and symmetry, adaptation to the reconstituted family requires an extra effort. When brothers with different parents are brought together into the same extended family, even if they are not necessarily cohabiting, new issues will have to be faced. These are bonds that are not chosen, imposed bonds, we might say, but bonds that must be shared. And what if the new siblings are smarter, or more interesting, or more affectionate? How can they be liked or loved? How can they *not* be liked or loved—and then how can this be expressed? And if there is mutual or unilateral rejection? How to make agreements? How to be open and receptive to affection, and how to negotiate it? How to reposition oneself in a new group of people? How to live and accommodate new arrangements and new dialogues?

We know that the fraternal bond has its own characteristics, as singular as they are evident, and that in general we are siblings for longer than we are children. Fraternal bonds can be stronger than those of parental relations. We also know that fraternal bonds are more exposed to rupture and detachment.

Nevertheless, we can finally conclude that *fratria* is always an experience of a great intimacy that was not chosen but imposed by parents, both in the original family as well in the reconstituted family. *Fratria,* the experience of brotherhood/sisterhood in both the constituted and the reconstituted family, will always mean, more than anything else, sharing memories. It is a lifelong task.